ON THE PRIESTHOOD

ON THE PRIESTHOOD
Classic and Contemporary Texts

Edited by
Matthew Levering

ROWMAN & LITTLEFIELD PUBLISHERS, INC.
Lanham • Boulder • New York • Oxford

ROWMAN & LITTLEFIELD PUBLISHERS, INC.

Published in the United States of America
by Rowman & Littlefield Publishers, Inc.
A Member of the Rowman & Littlefield Publishing Group
4501 Forbes Boulevard, Suite 200, Lanham, Maryland 20706
www.rowmanlittlefield.com

PO Box 317
Oxford
OX2 9RU, UK

British Library Cataloguing in Publication Information Available

Library of Congress Cataloging-in-Publication Data

On the priesthood : classic and contemporary texts / edited by Matthew
Levering
    p. cm.
Includes bibliographical references and index.
  ISBN 0-7425-1494-3 (alk. paper) — ISBN 0-7425-1495-1 (pbk. : alk.
paper)
  1. Priesthood—History of doctrines. 2. Priesthood—Catholic
Church—History of doctrines. I. Levering, Matthew Webb, 1971–
BX1912.048 2003
262'.1—dc21

                                                        2003006000

Printed in the United States of America

∞™ The paper used in this publication meets the minimum requirements of
American National Standard for Information Sciences—Permanence of Paper
for Printed Library Materials, ANSI/NISO Z39.48-1992.

To Fr. John J. Connelly and
Fr. Edward Mahoney

Contents

Introduction

WHAT DOES IT MEAN to be a priest, a bishop, or Pope? This book seeks to answer the question by listening attentively to some of the renowned teachers of the Church throughout the ages.

The authors included in this collection knew well the mystery of the simultaneous unworthiness and dignity of the priests of the New Covenant, who in receiving the sacrament of holy orders are anointed by Christ, through the power of the Holy Spirit, to guide, govern, and sanctify his flock, the Church. Jesus was well aware of the unworthiness of the disciples whom he himself had dignified: "Did I not choose you, the twelve, and one of you is a devil?" (Jn 6:70). After all, he chose the twelve from among his followers not randomly, but after a night spent in prayer: "In these days he went out into the hills to pray; and all night he continued in prayer to God. And when it was day, he called his disciples, and he chose from them twelve, whom he named apostles; Simon, whom he named Peter, and Andrew his brother, and James and John, and Philip, and Bartholomew, and Matthew, and Thomas, and James the son of Alphaeus, and Simon who was called the Zealot, and Judas the son of James, and Judas Iscariot, who became a traitor" (Lk 6:12–16). By selecting Judas, Jesus makes particularly clear that God intends for his Church to accomplish her mission of spreading the good news and sanctifying humankind by means of the work of sinful human beings.

Indeed, as St. John reminds us, "If we say we have no sin, we deceive ourselves, and the truth is not in us. If we confess our sins, he is faithful and just, and will forgive our sins and cleanse us from all unrighteousness. If we say we have not sinned, we make him a liar, and his word is not in us" (1 Jn 1:8–9). God works through sinners because we are all sinners. Through faith and repentence, we receive God's mercy and are united to Christ in his Church, yet we remain sinners. St. John continues, "My little children, I am writing this to you so that you may not sin; but if any one does sin, we have an advocate with the Father, Jesus Christ the righteous; and he is the expiation for our sins, and not for ours only but also for the sins of the whole world" (1 Jn 2:1–2).

And yet, when at times Jesus' own chosen ministers sin against him—as does not only Judas, but Peter himself—one might wonder whether Jesus was right to give to his Church a ministerial priesthood. If men are so unworthy, why does Jesus grant them the dignity of representing him sacramentally (*in persona Christi*, the Eucharistic center of the priestly vocation) to sanctify God's people?

In fact, this question does not merely address the priestly vocation. Rather, it cuts to the very heart of the Christian life. If we all—priests and laity—are unworthy, why does God so dignify us by sending his Son into the world for the forgiveness of our sins? Why does God so dignify us by making himself present to us in the Eucharist and in the other sacraments of our salvation? Why does God permit *any* of us, unworthy as we are, to bear the name "Christian," either the common priesthood of the laity or the ministerial priesthood of those who have received the sacrament of orders? Peter himself, amazed by witnessing one of Jesus' miracles early in Jesus' ministry, poignantly and powerfully articulates this profound concern: "Depart from me, for I am a sinful man, O Lord!" (Lk 5:8) St. Paul says, equally powerfully, "Why, one will hardly die for a righteous man—though perhaps for a good man one will dare even to die. But God shows his love for us in that while we were yet sinners Christ died for us" (Rom. 5:7–8). Christ calls us all to holiness, and yet we so often fall short.

The amazing reality is that God actually wills to give himself and his truth—the good news of the gospel—into the hands of sinful human beings. Through *sinful* human beings, God wills to communicate his *holy* truth and his *holy* presence, which sanctify us. This mystery is at the very core of what it means to be Catholic: We receive Christ's holiness, the grace of his Holy Spirit, through the mediation of other fallen human beings in the Church. Even though the Church's members on earth are sinners, the Church is holy, because God's holy teaching and holy presence dwells in the Church: as Jesus says of the Church, "the powers of death shall not prevail against it" (Mt 16:18). Jesus promises to strengthen his disciples by sending the Holy Spirit upon the Church, led by the twelve: "But the Counselor, the Holy Spirit, whom the Father will send in my name, he will teach you all things, and bring to your remembrance all that I have said to you" (Jn 14:26).

For this reason, despite her sinful members, the Church can be at peace that she indeed embodies—*by God's merciful power, not its own*—Christ's Wisdom for the world: "Peace I leave with you; my peace I give to you; not as the world gives do I give to you. Let not your hearts be troubled, neither let them be afraid" (Jn 14:27). Indeed, the risen Lord, who sends his Spirit upon the Church, mercifully upholds the Church in all ages by his truth and presence, enabling the Church to witness faithfully to God's merciful love despite her continual need for spiritual renewal. As Jesus tells his disciples after his resurrection, "All authority in heaven and on earth has been given to me. Go therefore and make disciples of all nations, baptizing them in the name of the Father and of the Son and of the Holy Spirit, teaching them to observe all that I have commanded you; and lo, I am with you always, to the close of the age" (Mt 28:18–20).

After his resurrection, Jesus specially strengthens Peter in love and holiness for his mission of shepherding the whole Church on earth: "When they had finished breakfast, Jesus said to Simon Peter, 'Simon, son of John, do you love me more than these?' He said to him, 'Yes, Lord; you know that I love you.' He said to him, 'Feed my lambs.' A second time he said to him, 'Simon, son of John, do you love me?' He said to him, 'Yes, Lord; you know that I love you.' He said to him, 'Tend my sheep.' He said to him the third time, 'Simon, son of John, do you love me?' And he said to him, 'Lord, you know everything; you know that I love you.' Jesus said to him, 'Feed my sheep.' . . . And after this he said to him, 'Follow me'" (Jn 21:15–17, 19). Peter's three confessions of faith reverse his three denials of Jesus before Jesus' crucifixion, and signify his repentance and his sanctification. In Jesus' relationship with Peter, we see the mystery of the unworthiness and the special dignity of the ministerial priest. The sanctifying of the flock—"feeding" and "tending" in truth and charity—constitutes the task for which Christ strengthens his ministerial priesthood, led by Peter.

In seeking to understand the priesthood, Christians may err in two ways: by focusing exclusively upon priests' great dignity as called by Christ to a special task, or by focusing exclusively upon their unworthiness as fallen human beings. Both aspects must be kept in mind if the true vocation of the ministerial priesthood in the Church is to be understood. As an example of a misguided idealization of the priestly vocation, focusing solely upon its dignity, a humorous episode of the television sitcom *Cheers*, set in a Boston bar, comes to mind. Carla, a longtime waitress at the bar, comes to work one day joyfully announcing that her son has decided to become a priest. However, this announcement does not spark in Carla a new commitment to Jesus' commandment to love others as he loved us, in other words, to her vocation as a member of the common priesthood. On the contrary, Carla uses the opportunity to take out her frustrations upon her co-workers and the patrons of the bar. After she verbally abuses a customer, she gleefully tells a co-worker that she can do anything she wants now: having a son as a priest is equivalent to having a "get-out-of-jail-free card." God, she argues, would never send to Hell the mother of one of God's priests.

Carla rightly responds joyfully to the possibility that Christ has called her son to the ministerial priesthood. Her mistake consists not in her high regard for the sanctifying mission of the ministerial priesthood, but rather in her assumption that her son's vocation will cancel out her own need, as a member of the common priesthood, to pursue holiness. Of course, Carla gets her deserved comeuppance. After she has treated almost everyone in the bar rudely, her son comes into the bar and reports that he has decided after all not to enter the priesthood. If memory serves, Carla sadly makes plans to go to confession!

If Carla embodies one end of the spectrum, on the other end one finds people who focus exclusively on the unworthiness of the ministerial priesthood and argue that priests are such sinners that the Church cannot be Christ's Church. Even the briefest glance at Church history reveals that priests—like laity—have always been sinners (could it be otherwise?). In all time periods some priests, like some laity, have committed terrible sins. Church history makes clear that Christ truly works in history through sinners (as well as powerfully through saints—that is, repentant sinners), despite the ever-present temptation of Christians to imagine that Christ's visible Church should contain only the purest of the pure.

The Church, composed of sinners, has always been in need of spiritual renewal, which is distinct from doctrinal development. For example, the first general Council of the Church, the Council of Nicea in A.D. 325, is renowned for proclaiming the truth of the Son's full divinity and full equality with the Father. The same Council, however, saw fit to suspend from active ministry priests who had castrated themselves, and also warns priests who had been charging usury and making a profit on their flocks. The Council also states about priests who have not received proper formation: "If with the passage of time some sin of sensuality is discovered with regard to the person and he is convicted by two or three witnesses, such a one will be suspended from the clergy." Further, the Council "absolutely forbids a bishop, presbyter, deacon or any of the clergy to keep a woman who has been brought in to live with him, with the exception of course of his mother or sister or aunt, or of any person who is above suspicion."[1] Clearly, some members of the priesthood, like some members of the laity, were already suffering from the scandal of sexual sins.

The mistake of focusing exclusively upon the unworthiness of priests does not mean that laity should not remind priests, in proper circumstances, of the universal call to holiness. Just like the laity, every priest, no matter how good, is always in need of being called to reform his life in accord with the radical demands of the gospel and thereby to avoid giving scandal. When the moral life of the laity is corrupt, it should come as no surprise to find that corruption also besets some members of the priesthood. Certain actions constitute scandalous sins against our neighbors and thus redound also upon our own spiritual well-being. As St. Paul puts it, "Do you not know that the unrighteous will not inherit the kingdom of God? Do not be deceived; neither the immoral, nor idolaters, nor adulterers, nor homosexuals, nor thieves, nor the greedy, nor drunkards, nor revilers, nor robbers will inherit the kingdom of God. And such were some of you" (1 Cor. 6:9–11). The Church's purpose, made possible by Christ's action through the Holy Spirit, consists in making fallen human beings holy, in charity governed by truth.

Granted, then, that the call to holiness and conversion is continually necessary, what is the root of the mistake made by those who focus exclusively on the unworthiness of priests? Essentially, such critics reason that since some priests, like some laity, are scandalously sinful, Christ would want nothing to do with this priesthood. Such critics are not only oblivious of all the great priests of today and of the past, but also are denying that God works through sinners. Without recognizing it, they implicitly deny that God could or would give himself, in Christ, into *our* hands—that is, they implicitly deny the very mystery of salvation. Admittedly, at times the scandal caused by God's gift of himself into the hands of sinful men can be hard to bear. Luther's dealings with Roman ecclesiastical authorities led him to conclude that the Pope "claims to be the head of the Christian Church, although he is a barefaced liar letting the Evil One dominate him. This arbitrary and deceptive 'mental reservation' on the part of the pope creates a state of affairs in Rome that beggars description. You can find there a buying and selling, a bartering and a bargaining, a lying and trickery, robbery and stealing, pomp, procuration, knavery, and all sorts of stratagems bringing God into contempt, till it would be impossible for the Antichrist to govern more wickedly."[2] Cardinal John Henry Newman himself believed for many years, while an Anglican, that the Pope was the Antichrist. Such claims, Newman came to realize, slanderously ignore the actual role that the popes have played in the development and proclamation of Catholic doctrine. The fact that popes are fallen human beings like the rest of us hardly precludes Christ, from whom all holiness comes, from working through them, and through the entire priesthood, to accomplish wonderful things.

This book contains a set of extraordinary discussions of the nature and character of the priesthood written by great Catholic saints and teachers from the twenty centuries of the Church's history. The fifteen selections strikingly illumine the way in which the ministerial priesthood nourishes the unity and holiness of the whole Church. The selections never shirk from engaging and addressing the problem of the personal failings of some of those who have shared in this ministry. On the contrary, the selections continually call for spiritual renewal rooted in penance and prayer.

In organizing the selections, I have divided the history of the Church into five major periods: Apostolic (from Pentecost to A.D. 160), Patristic (160–700), Medieval (700–1500), Reformation and Early Modern (1500–1800), and Modern (1800 to the present). The Apostolic section contains excerpts from the writings of St. Clement of Rome, the third bishop of Rome after St. Peter; St. Ignatius of Antioch, bishop of Antioch whose surviving letters were written while he was in chains and on his way to Rome to be pulled to pieces in the Coliseum for the crime of being Christian; and St. Polycarp of Smyrna, who knew the apostle John and was himself martyred by the Roman authorities, when in his eighties, for the crime of being Christian.

From the Patristic period, we learn the practical and ascetical advice of the great bishops St. John Chrysostom, who was exiled for preaching sermons that challenged the leading men and women of Constantinople to a deeper holiness; St. Ambrose, who baptized St. Augustine; and St. Gregory the Great, who was called from his monastery to become Pope and who reformed the Church. From the Medieval period, we find the warnings against worldliness directed by St. Bernard of Clairvaux to the new Pope, a former monk in Bernard's monastery; meditations by St. Thomas Aquinas upon the Gospel of John, in which Aquinas examines the use and misuse of the pastoral office; and St. Catherine of Siena's extraordinary mystical writings on the dignity and corruption of the priesthood.

From the Reformation and Early Modern period, the need for priests to have a deep spiritual life is exposed and discussed by St. Thomas More, beheaded for refusing to accept the King's claim to rule the Church in England; by St. Jane de Chantal, the great associate of St. Francis de Sales in developing methods of spiritual renewal and a deepened life of prayer; and by Jean-Jacques Olier, who helped to found numerous seminaries in which the training of priests was reformed. Last, the Modern section includes a magnificent essay by Cardinal Newman on the nature of the priesthood; an excerpt from Vatican II's Dogmatic Constitution on the Church, *Lumen Gentium*, in which the particular structure and duties of the priesthood are set forth; and a beautiful excerpt from Pope John Paul II's meditation on the priestly vocation on the fiftieth anniversary of his ordination.

In these selections, one sees the vocation of the priest described not only theoretically but also in the practical details of everyday life. One learns about the duties and authority of the priesthood, as well as about how and when to call to account unworthy priests. The great teachers of the Church have never thought of priests as more than human. Neither have they denied the real dignity and legitimate authority of the priestly office. By listening to the diverse voices contained in this collection of magnificent writings, one can arrive at a sane, balanced, and appreciative view of the priestly vocation in the Church that includes its aspects of evangelization, teaching, governance, and, above all, *holiness.*

From the twelve apostles chosen by Jesus all the way to his priests of today, this book thus provides a reliable and inspiring guide for bishops, priests, seminarians, and laity who desire to seek deeper insight, from the heart of the Church, into the meaning of priesthood today. Guided by the profound writings of the men and women in this book, we will enter more fully into the truth that God, willing to reconcile all things to himself in Christ Jesus, has chosen—in Cardinal Newman's succinct phrase—"men, not angels, the priests of the gospel."

Notes

1. Norman P. Tanner, S.J., ed., *Decrees of the Ecumenical Councils*, vol. 1 (Washington, D.C.: Georgetown University Press, 1990), 6–7,14 (canons 1–3,17).

2. From Martin Luther, "An Appeal to the Ruling Class of German National-ity as to the Amelioration of the State of Christendom," in John Dillenberger, ed., *Martin Luther: Selections from His Writings* (New York: Anchor Books, 1962), 429.

St. Clement of Rome

St. Clement, the third successor to St. Peter as the bishop of Rome, served in the late first century (approximately A.D. 90–99). He wrote to the Corinthians in response to a schism in which some members of the Corinthian church had rejected the authority of the Corinthian priesthood. In this excerpt we find St. Clement's theologically erudite plea for the Corinthian church to be united under the authority of the ministerial priesthood, in accord with Christ's will. Against the schismatics, St. Clement emphasizes that the ministerial priesthood promotes the true unity that is found in imitation of Christ through obedience, humility, and charity.

THIS IS THE WAY, beloved, by which we found our Saviour, Jesus Christ, the high priest[1] of our offerings, the protector and the helper of our weakness. Through Him let us strain our eyes toward the heights of heaven; through Him we see mirrored His spotless and glorious countenance.[2] Through Him the eyes of our heart have been opened; through Him our foolish and darkened understanding shoots up into the light; through Him the Lord willed that we should taste immortal knowledge, "Who, being the brightness of his majesty is so much greater than the angels as he hath inherited a more excellent name."[3] For it is so written:[4]

From: "The Letter to the Corinthians," trans. Francis X. Glimm, Fathers of the Church Series, ed. Ludwig Schopp, vol. 1: *The Apostolic Fathers* (Washington, D.C.: The Catholic University of America Press, 1947), 38–50.

"Who makes his angels spirits, and his ministers a flame of fire." But regarding His Son the Lord has spoken thus:[5] "Thou art My Son; this day I have begotten Thee. Ask of Me, and I will give Thee the gentiles for Thy inheritance, and the end of the earth for Thy possession." And again He says to Him:[6] "Sit on My right hand until I make Thy enemies a footstool for Thy feet." Who then are the enemies? They are who wicked and resist His will.

Brothers, let us be His soldiers, therefore, in all earnestness, under His faultless commands. Let us consider those who are enrolled under our rulers, how well-ordered, and how readily, how obediently they carry out commands. Not all are prefects, or tribunes, or centurions, or in charge of bands of fifty, and so forth; but each one in his own rank[7] carries out the commands issued by the emperor and the officers. The great cannot exist without the small, nor the small without the great; there is a certain organization, and it is of benefit to all. Let us take our body.[8] The head without the feet is nothing, and so also the feet without the head are nothing. The smallest members of our body are necessary and useful to the whole body. But all conspire together and unite in a single obedience, so that the whole body may be saved.

Therefore, let our whole body be saved in Christ Jesus, and let each be subject to his neighbor, according to the position which grace bestowed on each.[9] Let not the strong neglect the weak, and let the weak respect the strong. Let the rich man supply the wants of the poor, and let the poor man give thanks to God, because He has given him someone to supply his needs. Let the wise show his wisdom not in words, but in good works. Let the humble-minded not testify to his own humility, but allow others to bear him witness. Let him who is pure in the flesh be so without boasting, knowing that it is Another who grants him this continence. Let us consider, brothers, of what matter we were made; who and what we are who have come into the world; from what a tomb and what darkness our Maker and Creator brought us into the world and prepared His benefits for us before we were born. We who have obtained all these things from Him ought to thank Him for all, to whom be glory forever and ever. Amen.

Foolish, unthinking, silly, and ignorant men laugh at us and deride us, wishing to exalt themselves in their own imagination. For what can mortal man do? Or what is the strength of one born on earth? For it is written:[10] "There was no shape before my eyes, but I heard breathing and a voice. What then? Shall a mortal be pure before the Lord? Or shall a man be blameless in his works [before God], if He believeth not in His servants, and finds defects in His angels? Even the heaven is not pure in His sight. Away, you that live in houses of clay, from which, yes, from the same clay, we ourselves were made. He struck them like a moth, and between morning and evening they ceased to exist; they perished without being able to help themselves. He breathed on them, and they died, because they had not wisdom. Cry out, if there is anyone to hear thee; or if thou shalt see any of the holy angels. For wrath destroyeth the foolish man, and jealousy kills him that errs. I have seen the foolish take root, but shortly their dwelling was consumed. Let their sons be far from safety; let them be derided in the gates of their inferiors, and there will be none to rescue them. For the just shall eat what was prepared for them, and they shall not be delivered from their ills."

Since all these things are clear to us, and we have looked into the depths of divine knowledge,[11] we ought in proper order to do all things which the Lord has commanded us to perform at appointed times. He has commanded the offerings and ministrations to be carried out, and not carelessly or disorderly, but at fixed times and seasons. He has Himself fixed according to His surpassing counsel where and by whom He desires them to be performed, in order that all things may be done in holy fashion according to His good pleasure and acceptable to His will. Those who make their offerings at the appointed time, therefore, are acceptable and blessed, for they err not, following the ordinances of the Lord. For the high priest has been allotted his proper ministrations, and to the priests their proper place has been assigned, and on the Levites their own duties are laid. The lay man is bound by the lay ordinances.

Let us, brothers, each in his own order,[12] strive to please God with a good conscience and with reverence, not transgressing the fixed rule of each one's own ministry. Not in every place, brothers, are the daily sacrifices for petitions and for sins and for trespasses offered, but only in Jerusalem. And even there the offering is not made in any place, but only before the sanctuary near the altar, after the offering has been inspected for defects by the high priest and the above-mentioned ministers. Those who do anything contrary to what is due to Him will suffer the penalty of death. You see, brothers, the more knowledge we have been given, the more we are exposed to danger.

The Apostles received the Gospel for us from the Lord Jesus Christ; Jesus Christ was sent from God. Christ, therefore, is from God and the

Apostles are from Christ. Both, accordingly, came in proper order by the will of God. Receiving their orders, therefore, and being filled with confidence because of the Resurrection of the Lord Jesus Christ, and confirmed in the word of God, with full assurance of the Holy Spirit, they went forth preaching the Gospel of the Kingdom of God that was about to come. Preaching, accordingly, throughout the country and the cities, they appointed their first-fruits, after testing them by the Spirit, to be bishops and deacons of those who should believe. And this they did without innovation, since many years ago things had been written concerning bishops and deacons. Thus, the Scripture says in one place:[13] "I will establish their bishops in justice and their deacons in faith."

And what wonder is it if they, who had been entrusted in Christ by God with such a work, appointed the persons we have mentioned? After all, the blessed man Moses, "a faithful servant in all his house,"[14] recorded in the sacred books all the things commanded him. And the other prophets followed him, testifying with him to the laws laid down by him. For, when jealousy arose about the priesthood[15] and the tribes quarreled as to which of them should be honored with that glorious name, he commanded the chiefs of the twelve tribes to bring him rods inscribed with the name of each tribe; and, taking them, he bound them, and sealed them with the rings of the chiefs, and put them away in the Tabernacle of Testimony on the table of God. And, closing the Tabernacle of Testimony, he sealed the keys as well as the doors. And he said to them: "Brethren, the tribe whose rod blossoms, this one has God chosen to be priests and to minister to Him." And, when morning came, he called together all Israel, six hundred thousand men, and showed the seals to the chiefs of the tribes, and opened the Tabernacle of Testimony, and brought out the rods; and the rod of Aaron was found not only to have blossomed, but also to be bearing fruit. What do you think, beloved? Did not Moses know beforehand that this would happen? Certainly, he knew. But, that no disorder should arise in Israel, he acted thus to glorify the name of the true and only God, to whom be glory forever and ever. Amen.

Our Apostles also knew, through our Lord Jesus Christ, that there would be contention over the bishop's office. So, for this cause, having received complete foreknowledge, they appointed the above-mentioned men, and afterwards gave them a permanent character, so that, as they died, other approved men should succeed to their ministry. Those, therefore, who were appointed by the Apostles or afterwards by other

eminent men, with the consent of the whole Church, and who ministered blamelessly to the flock of Christ in humility, peaceably and nobly,
being commended for many years by all—these men we consider are not
justly deposed from their ministry. It will be no small sin for us, if we depose from the episcopacy men who have blamelessly and in holiness offered up sacrifice. Blessed are the presbyters who have gone before, since
they reached a fruitful and perfect end; for now they need not fear that
anyone shall remove them from the place assigned to them. For we see
that, in spite of their good conduct, you have forced some men from a
ministry which they fulfilled without blame.

Brothers, be eager and zealous for the things that pertain to salvation.
You have studied the Holy Scriptures, which are true and inspired by the
Holy Spirit. You know that nothing contrary to justice or truth has been
written in them. You will not find that just men have been expelled by
holy men. Just men were persecuted, but by wicked men. They were im-
prisoned, but by impious men. They were stoned by breakers of the laws;
they were killed by men who had conceived a foul and wicked jealousy.
Although suffering such things, they endured nobly. What shall we say,
brothers? Was Daniel cast into the lions' den by men who feared God?[16]
Or were Ananias, Azarias, and Misael shut up in the fiery furnace by
men who observed the great and glorious worship of the Most High?
God forbid! Who, then, were the men who did these acts? They were detestable men, filled with all wickedness, who were carried to such fury
that they heaped humiliation on those who served God in holiness and
purity of intention. They did not know that the Most High is the protector and defender of those who minister with a pure conscience to His
all holy Name, to whom be glory forever and ever. Amen. But those who
endured confidently gained an inheritance of glory and honor, and were
exalted and inscribed by God in His memorial forever and ever. Amen.

And so, brothers, we, too, must cling to models such as these. For it is
written:[17] "Cling to the saints, for they who cleave to them shall become
saints." And again in another place:[18] "With the innocent man, Thou
shalt be innocent; and with the elect man, Thou shalt be elect; and with
the perverse man, Thou shalt be perverse." Let us cling, then, to the innocent and the just, for they are God's elect. Why are there quarrels and
ill will and dissensions and schism and fighting among you? Do we not
have one God and one Christ, and one Spirit of Grace poured out upon
us? And is there not one calling in Christ?[19] Why do we wrench and tear

apart the members of Christ, and revolt against our own body, and reach such folly as to forget that we are members one of another? Remember the words of the Lord Jesus: For He said:[20] "Woe to that man! It were better for him if he had not been born, rather than scandalize one of My elect. It were better for him that a millstone were tied to him, and that he be cast into the sea, than he should pervert one of My chosen ones." Your schism has perverted many, has thrown many into despair, has caused all of us to grieve; and your rebelliousness continues.

Take up the epistle of blessed Paul the Apostle.[21] What did he first write to you at the beginning of his preachings?[22] In truth, being inspired, he wrote to you concerning himself and Cephas and Apollos, because even then you were given to faction. But that factiousness involved you in less guilt, for you were partisans of highly reputed Apostles, and of a man commended by them. But consider now who they are who have perverted you, and have diminished the honor of your renowned reputation for brotherly love. It is disgraceful, beloved, very disgraceful, and unworthy of your training in Christ, to hear that the stable and ancient Church of the Corinthians, on account of one or two persons, should revolt against its presbyters. And this report has come not only to us, but also to those who dissent from us. The result is that blasphemies are brought upon the name of the Lord through your folly, and danger accrues for yourselves.

Let us quickly remove this, then, and let us fall down before the Lord and supplicate Him with tears that He may become merciful and be reconciled to us, and restore us to the honored and holy practice of brotherly love. For thus is the gate of justice opened to life, as it is written:[23] "Open to me the gates of justice, that I may enter through them and praise the Lord. This is the gate of the Lord, the righteous shall enter by it." Of the many gates that are opened, the one in justice is the one in Christ. All are blessed who enter by this gate and pursue their way in holiness and justice, performing all things without disorder.[24] Let a man be faithful, let him be able to utter deep knowledge, let him be wise in discerning words, let him be energetic in deeds,[25] let him be pure. For the greater he seems to be, so much the more should he be humble; and he ought to seek the common good of all and not his own.

Let him who has chastity in Christ keep Christ's commandments. Who can explain the bond of the charity of God?[26] Who can express the splendor of its beauty? The height to which charity lifts us is inexpressible. Charity unites us to God, "charity covers a multitude of sins";[27] charity bears all things, is long-suffering in all things. There is nothing mean in charity, nothing arrogant. Charity knows no schism, does not rebel, does all things in concord. In charity all the elect of God have been made perfect. Without charity nothing is pleasing to God. In charity the Lord received us; out of charity which He had for us, Jesus Christ our Lord gave his blood for us by the will of God, and His flesh for our flesh, and His life for our lives.

You see, dearly beloved, how great and wonderful is charity, and that its perfection is beyond expression. Who is good enough to be found in it except those whom God makes worthy? Let us pray, therefore, and beg of His mercy that we may be found in charity, without human partisanship, free from blame. All the generations from Adam to this day have passed away; but those who were made perfect in charity by the grace of God live among the saints; and they shall be made manifest at the judgment of the Kingdom of Christ. For it is written:[28] "Enter into thy chambers a little while, until My wrath and anger pass, and I remember the good day and will raise you up out of your graves." Blessed were we, dearly beloved, if we fulfilled the commandments of God in the harmony of charity, that our sins were forgiven through charity. For it is written:[29] "Blessed are they whose iniquities are forgiven, and whose sins are covered. Blessed is the man whose sin the Lord will not reckon, and in whose mouth there is no deceit." This benediction came to those who were chosen by God through Jesus Christ our Lord, to whom be glory forever and ever. Amen.

Whatsoever we have done wrong, and whatsoever we have done by suggestion of our adversary, let us hope that it may be forgiven us. Even those who were the leaders of rebellion and schism must look to the common hope. For those who live in fear and charity prefer that they, rather than their neighbors, should undergo sufferings, and they more willingly suffer their own condemnation than the loss of that harmony which has been taught us well and justly. It is better for a man to confess his sins than to harden his heart, as the heart of those who rebelled against Moses, then servant of God who was hardened[30]—and the verdict on them was plain. For they went "down into Hades alive" and "death will gather them in."[31] Pharaoh and his army and all the leaders of Egypt, "the chariots and their riders," were drowned in the Red Sea and perished, for no other reason than that their foolish hearts were hardened, after the working of signs and wonders in the land of Egypt by God's servant Moses.[32]

Brothers, the Lord of the universe has need of nothing; He requires nothing of anyone, except that confession be made to Him. For David, the chosen one, says:[33] "I will confess to the Lord, and it shall please Him more than a young bullock with horns and hoofs. Let the poor see it and be glad." And again he says:[34] "Sacrifice to God a sacrifice of praise, and render to the All-High thy vows; and call upon Me in the day of affliction, and I will deliver thee, and thou shalt glorify Me." "For a contrite spirit is a sacrifice to God."[35]

For you understand, beloved, you well understand the Sacred Scriptures, and you have studied the oracles of God. So we write these things as a reminder. For, when Moses went up the mountain and spent forty days and forty nights in fasting and humiliation, God said to him:[36] "Go down from here quickly, for thy people, whom thou has brought out of Egypt, have committed iniquity; they have speedily gone astray from the way which thou hast commanded them; they have made molten images for themselves." And the Lord said to him:[37] "I have spoken to thee once and twice, saying, 'I have seen this people, and, behold, it is stiff-necked. Suffer Me to destroy them and I will wipe out their name from under heaven, and I will make thee a great and wonderful nation, far more numerous than this one.' And Moses said:[38] 'No Lord; pardon the sin of this people, or blot me also out of the book of the living.'" What great charity! What superb perfection! The servant speaks out to the Lord and asks that the people be forgiven or that he himself be blotted out with them.

Who, now, among you is noble? Who is compassionate? Who is filled with charity? Let him say: "If on my account there are sedition and quarreling and schisms, I will leave; I will go wherever you wish and will do what is enjoined by the community, only let the flock of Christ have peace with its appointed presbyters." He who does this will win for himself great fame in Christ, and every place will receive him, for "the earth is the Lord's, and the fullness of it."[39] Thus have they acted and will continue to act who fulfill their obligations as citizens of God without regret.

Questions for Clement

1. Why does Clement think that Christian humility is assisted by the Church's hierarchical structure?

2. What are, according to Clement, the "ordinances" of the Lord? How are these related to charity (love)?

3. Does Clement think that the Apostles expected contention over the bishop's office? About what did St. Paul write to the Corinthians?

Notes

1. Heb. 2:18; 3:1.
2. Cf. 2 Cor. 3:18.
3. Heb. 1:3,4.
4. Ps. 103:94; Heb. 1:7.
5. Ps. 2:7,8; Heb. 1:5.
6. Ps. 109:1; Heb. 1:13.
7. 1 Cor. 15:23.
8. For the following passage cf. 1 Cor. 12.
9. Cf. Rom. 12:4 ff.; 1 Cor. 16:17; Phil. 2:30.
10. Job 4:12–18; 15:15; 4:19–5:5.
11. Rom. 11:33.
12. 1 Cor. 15:23.
13. Isa. 60:17. This is a free adaptation of the text by St. Clement. The Septuagint reads: "I will establish your rulers in peace and your overseers (*episkopous*) in justice."
14. Num. 12:7; Heb. 3:5.
15. Num. 17.
16. Dan. 6:16,17; 3:19 ff.
17. Source unknown.
18. Cf. Ps. 17:26,27.
19. Eph. 4:4-6.
20. Matt. 26:24; Luke 17:1,2; Mark 9:42.
21. 1 Cor. 1:10 ff.
22. Phil. 4:15.
23. Ps. 117:19,20.
24. Luke 1:75.
25. Cf. 1 Cor. 12:8,9.
26. Cf. Col. 3:14.
27. Prov. 10:12; 1 Peter 4:8; James 5:20.
28. Isa. 26:20; Ezek. 37:12.
29. Ps. 31:1,2: Rom. 4:7–9.
30. Num. 16.

31. Num. 16:33; Ps. 48:15.
32. Exod. 14:23.
33. Ps. 68:31–33.
34. Ps. 49:14,15.
35. Ps. 50:19.
36. Deut. 9:12.
37. Deut. 9:13,14.
38. Exod. 32:31,32.
39. Ps. 23:1.

St. Ignatius of Antioch

St. Ignatius, Bishop of Antioch, wrote this letter around A.D. 110 while in chains. Because of his Christian faith, Roman soldiers were leading him to Rome to be thrown to the beasts in the Flavian amphitheatre and martyred. In this letter, he develops his profound concept of the Church as a symphony in which each member has a distinct note to sing, and all sing in unison the harmony of Jesus Christ. A key to the unity of this symphony, St. Ignatius teaches, is the authority of the bishops and priesthood. The goal of this harmonious symphony is the imitation of Christ by obedience, sustained by the reception of Christ in the Eucharist.

IGNATIUS THEOPHORUS GREETS the Church of Ephesus in Asia, congratulating you as you deserve and wishing you perfect joy in Jesus Christ—you who have grown in spiritual stature through the fullness of God the Father, and have been predestined from eternity to eternal abiding and unchanging glory, and have been united and chosen through a true passion by the will of the Father and of Jesus Christ, our God.

I have welcomed in God your well beloved name, which is yours by reason of your natural goodness in accord with faith and charity in Jesus Christ, our Savior. Imitators of God as you are, with hearts warmed in

"The Letter to the Ephesians," trans. Gerald G. Walsh, S.J., Fathers of the Church Series, ed. Ludwig Schopp, vol. 1: *The Apostolic Fathers* (Washington, D.C.: The Catholic University of America Press, 1947), 87–95.

the blood of God, you have done perfectly the work that fell to you to do; for you were eager to visit me when you heard that I was on my way from Syria, in chains because of our common name and hope, and longing, with the help of your prayers, to face the wild beasts in Rome and not to fail and so become a disciple. And so in God's name I received your whole community in the person of Onesimus, your bishop, in the flesh, a man whose charity is beyond all power to say. I beg of you to love him in Jesus Christ and to be like him to a man. May He be blessed who gave you the grace to have and to deserve to have such a bishop.

A word about Burrhus, my fellow worker and your deacon by the will of God, a man blessed in every way. It is my prayer that he may continue with me to your honor and that of your bishop. Crocus, too, who is worthy of God and of yourselves, I have received as an exemplar of the love you bear me. He has been a great comfort to me in every way. May the Father of Jesus Christ reward him with His grace—and not only him but Onesimus, Burrhus, Euplus and Fronto; for in them I saw the love of all of you. If only I deserve it, may I have joy in you always. And so it is right for you to glorify Jesus Christ in every way, who has given you glory so that you may be made perfect in a single obedience to your bishop and the priests and be made holy in every way.

I do not give you orders as though I were a person of importance, for I have not yet been made perfect in Jesus Christ, even though I am a prisoner for His name. But, at last, I am beginning to be His disciple and speak to you as His disciples, too. For I have need of being trained by you faith, counsel, endurance and long-suffering. Still, love will not let me be silent in your regard, and so I make bold to beg you to be in harmony with God's mind. For Jesus Christ, the life that cannot be taken from us, is the mind of the Father, and the bishops appointed to ends of the earth are of one mind with Jesus Christ.

Hence, it is right for you to concur, as you do, with the name of the bishop. For your priests, who are worthy of the name and worthy of God, like the strings of a lyre, are in harmony with the bishops. Hence it is that in the harmony of your minds and hearts Jesus Christ is hymned. Make of yourselves a choir, so that with one voice and one mind, taking the key-note to God, you may sing in unison with one voice through Jesus Christ to the Father, and He may hear you and recognize you, in your good works, as members of His son. It is good for you, therefore, to be in perfect unity that you may at all times be partakers of God.

And if I, in a short time, have achieved such spiritual and not merely human communion with your bishop, all the more do I congratulate you who have become one with him, as the Church is one with Jesus Christ and as Jesus Christ is one with the Father, so that all things may be in harmony. Let no man be deceived. If a person is not inside the sanctuary[1] he is deprived of the Bread. For if the prayer of one or two men[2] has so much force, how much greater is that of the bishop and of the whole Church. Any one, therefore, who fails to assemble with the others has already shown his pride and set himself apart. For it is written: "God resists the proud."[3] Let us be careful, therefore, not to oppose the bishop, so that we may be obedient to God.

And let a man respect the bishop all the more if he sees him to be a man of few words. For, whoever is sent by the Master to run His house, we ought to receive him as we would receive the Master himself. It is obvious, therefore, that we ought to regard the bishop as we would the Lord Himself. I should tell you that Onesimus himself is full of praise for your orderly, religious behavior, because all of you are living according to truth and because among you no heresy finds a home. Indeed, you do not so much as listen to anyone unless his speech is of Jesus Christ in truth.

There are some who, in guile and wickedness, have a way of bearing the Name about while behaving in a way unworthy of God. Such men you must shun as you would wild beasts; for they are mad dogs that bite when you are not on your guard. Of these you must beware, for these men are hard to heal. There is one Doctor active in both body and soul, begotten and yet unbegotten, God in man, true life in death, son of Mary and Son of God, first able to suffer and then unable to suffer, Jesus Christ, our Lord.

Let no one, therefore, deceive you as, in fact, being wholly given to God, you are not deceived. For, so long as no passion within you has an established power to torment you, you are certainly living according to God. As a cheap sacrifice in your stead I offer myself for you Ephesians, for your Church which will be remembered in every age. Carnal men can no more do the works of the spirit than those who walk in the spirit do the things of the flesh; nor can faith do the things of infidelity nor infidelity the things of faith. Since you do all things in Jesus Christ, even those things are spiritual which you do according to the flesh.

I have learned that some strangers holding bad doctrine have passed your way, but that you have not allowed them to sow their seed among you and have stopped your ears lest you should receive what they sowed. Like the stones of a temple, cut for a building of God the Father, you have been lifted up to the top by the crane of Jesus Christ, which is the Cross, and the rope of the Holy Spirit. For your faith has drawn you up and charity has been the road leading to God. You are all fellow pilgrims, carrying with you God and His temple; you are bearers of Christ and of holy offerings, decked out in the commandments of Jesus Christ. And with this letter I am able to take part in your festivity, to be of your company, to share in the joy that comes from setting your heart not on what is merely human life, but on God.

And so do not cease to pray for all other men, for there is hope of their conversion and of their finding God. Give them the chance to be instructed, at least by the way you behave. When they are angry with you, be meek; answer their words of pride by your humility, their blasphemies by your prayers, their error by your steadfastness in faith, their bullying by your gentleness. Let us not be in a hurry to give them tit for tat, but, by our sweet reasonableness, show that we are their brothers. Let us rather be eager to imitate the Lord, striving to be the first in bearing wrongs, in suffering loss, in being despised, so that no weed of the evil one may be found among you; but abide in Jesus Christ in perfect purity and temperance of body and soul.

The last days are at hand. For the rest, let us live in reverence and fear of the patience of God, lest it turn in judgment against us. Either let us fear the wrath which is to come or else let us love the grace we have—one or the other, so long as we are found in Jesus Christ unto true life. Let nothing appeal to you apart from Him, by whose help I bear my chains about with me like spiritual pearls; and in these, with your prayers—in which I trust always to have a share—may I rise again, so that I may be found in the company of the Christian Ephesians who have always been at one with the Apostles through the power of Jesus Christ.

I know who I am and to whom I am writing. I am a condemned man; you have received mercy. I am in danger; you are safe. You are the road for those on the way to die for God. You have shared in the sacraments with Paul who was made a saint, who died a martyr, who deserved to be blessed—in whose footsteps may I be found when I reach God; in whose every letter there is a mention of you in Christ Jesus.

Be zealous, therefore, to assemble more frequently to render thanks[4] and praise to God. For, when you meet together frequently, the powers of Satan are destroyed and danger from him is dissolved in the harmony of your faith. There is nothing better than peace in which an end is put to the warfare of things in heaven and on earth.

You are aware of all these truths if you have perfect faith and love for Jesus Christ—the beginning and end of life; for faith is the beginning and the end is the love and God is the two of them brought into unity. After these comes whatever else makes up a Christian gentleman. No one commits sin who professes the faith, and no one hates who is possessed of charity. A tree is shown by its fruit,[5] and in the same way those who profess to belong to Christ will be seen by what they do. For what is needed is not mere present profession, but perseverance to the end in the power of faith.

It is better to say nothing and be than to speak and not to be. It is good to teach, if one practices what he preaches. There is one Teacher who spoke—and the thing was done;[6] and even the things He did without speaking are worthy of the Father. Anyone who is really possessed of the word of Jesus can listen to His silence and so be perfect; so that he may act through his words and be known by his silence. Nothing is hidden from the Lord and even the things we hide are near Him. Let us do all that we do, therefore, as though He were dwelling within us—we as His temple and He within as our God. And so, indeed, it is, and will be clearly seen by us from the love we justly bear Him.

Make no mistake, brethren; the corrupters of families will not inherit the kingdom of God. If, then, those are dead who do these things according to the flesh, how much worse if, with bad doctrine, one should corrupt the faith of God for which Jesus Christ was crucified. Such a man, for becoming contaminated, will depart into unquenchable fire; and so will anyone who listens to him.

It was for this reason that the Lord received the ointment on his head[7]—that he might breathe the odor of incorruptibility into the Church. Be not anointed with the bad odor of the doctrine of the prince of this world, lest he lead you away captive from the life proposed to you. Why do we not all become wise by accepting the knowledge of God which is Jesus Christ? Why do we perish in our folly by being ignorant of the grace which the Lord has truly sent us?

I offer up my life as a poor substitute for the Cross, which is a stumbling block to those who have no faith, but to us salvation and eternal life. Where is the wise man? Where is the philosopher?[8] Where is the boasting of the so-called men of prudence? For our God Jesus Christ was, according to God's dispensation, the fruit of Mary's womb, of the

seed of David; He was born and baptized in order that He might make
the water holy by His passion.

The maidenhood of Mary and her child-bearing and also the death of
the Lord were hidden from the prince of this world—three resounding
mysteries wrought in the silence of God. How, then, did He appear in
time? A star, brighter than all other stars, shone in the sky, and its brightness was ineffable and the novelty of it caused astonishment. And the
rest of the stars, along with the sun and the moon, formed a choir about
the star; but the light of the star by itself outshone all the rest. It was a
puzzle to know the origin of this novelty unlike anything else. There-
upon all magic was dissolved, every bond of malice disappeared, ignorance was destroyed, the ancient kingdom was ruined, when God appeared in the form of man to give us newness of eternal life. What had
been prepared in God now had a beginning. And, because of the plan for
the abolition of death, all things were disturbed.

If, through your prayers, Jesus Christ should make me worthy and if
it should be His will, and still more if the Lord should reveal it to me, in
a second letter which I intend to write to you, I shall explain more fully
what I have merely touched upon—the dispensation of becoming the
new man Jesus Christ, who is of the race of David according to the passion and resurrection. Come together in common, one and all without
exception in charity, in one faith and in one Jesus Christ, who is of the
race of David according to the flesh, the son of man and Son of God, so
that with undivided mind you may obey the bishop and the priests, and
break one Bread which is the medicine of immortality and the antidote
against death, enabling us to live for ever in Jesus Christ.

I am offering up my life for you and for those whom, to the honor of
God, you sent to Smyrna; and from here I write to you, thanking the
Lord and loving Polycarp as I love you. Remember me as Jesus Christ remembers you. Pray for the Church which is in Syria, from which I, the
last of the faithful there, am being led away a prisoner to Rome; for so I
was deemed worthy to be found to God's glory. Farewell in God the Father and in Jesus Christ our common hope.

Questions for Ignatius

1. How and why does the bishop, according to Ignatius, represent the
   whole community?

2. Describe the harmony that Ignatius envisions. What is the "Bread" that is under the charge of the bishop?

3. Is the bishop a man of "importance," as that term is commonly understood? What would it take in Ignatius's view to become "important"?

Notes

1. Literally, "the place of sacrifice."

2. Cf. Matt. 18:18–20.

3. Prov. 3:34.

4. The verb *eucharistein* may well have here the more special sense of "to celebrate the Eucharist."

5. Cf. Matt. 12:33; Luke 5:44.

6. Cf. Ps. 32:9.

7. Cf. John 12:3.

8. Cf. 1 Cor. 1:20,23,24.

St. Polycarp of Smyrna

St. Polycarp, Bishop of Smyrna and friend of St. Ignatius of Antioch, may have known St. John the Apostle. When he was eighty years of age, around A.D. 156, St. Polycarp died a martyr's death in a persecution of Christians in Smyrna. He wrote this letter to the Philippian Church around A.D. 110, near the time of St. Ignatius's death. The letter offers to the Philippians St. Polycarp's teachings on how to lead a virtuous Christian life and contains a warning to the priest Valens. Valens and his wife have fallen into a life of sin, and are no longer true followers of the eternal High Priest Jesus Christ.

POLYCARP AND THE PRESBYTERS who are with him to the Church of God dwelling at Philippi; may mercy and peace be richly increased in you from God Almighty and Jesus Christ our Savior.

I greatly rejoice with you in Lord Jesus Christ for having followed the pattern of true charity and for having escorted, as far as you could, those who were chained in saintly bonds; for they are the jewels of those who have been truly chosen by God and our Lord. And I rejoice because the firm root of your faith, famous in times past, still flourishes and bears fruit unto our Lord Jesus Christ, who for our sins endured to face even death. "Whom God had raised up, having broken the pangs of Hell."[1] In

"The Letter to the Philippians," trans. Francis X. Glimm, Fathers of the Church Series, ed. Ludwig Schopp, vol. 1: *The Apostolic Fathers* (Washington, D.C.: The Catholic University of America Press, 1947), 135–143.

Him, "though you see him not, you believe with unspeakable glorious joy,"[2] to which joy many desire to come, knowing that "by grace you are saved, not through works," but by the will of God through Jesus Christ.[3]

"Wherefore, girding up your loins, serve God in fear"[4] and in truth; abandon empty vanity and the waywardness of the crowd, "believing in Him who raised our Lord Jesus Christ from the dead and gave Him glory,"[5] and a throne at His right hand. "To Him are subject all things in Heaven and on earth," Him every breath serves and He will come as "the judge of the living and of the dead and His blood God will require from them who disobey Him."[6] Now "He who raised him" from the dead "will also raise us,"[7] if we do His will and advance in His commandments and love what He loved, abstaining from all injustice, covetousness, love of money, slander, false witness, "not rendering evil for evil, or abuse for abuse,"[8] or blow for blow, or curse for curse. No! Remember what the Lord said when he taught: "Judge not, that you may not be judged. Forgive, and you shall be forgiven. Be merciful, that you may obtain mercy. With what measure you measure, it shall be measured to you in return."[9] And again: "Blessed are the poor, and they who are persecuted for justice' sake, for theirs is the Kingdom of God."[10]

Brethren, I write you this concerning righteousness, not on my own initiative, but because you first invited me. For neither I, nor anyone like me, is able to rival the wisdom of the blessed and glorious Paul, who, when living among you, carefully and steadfastly taught the word of truth face to face with his contemporaries and, when he was absent, wrote you letters. By the careful perusal of his letters you will be able to strengthen yourselves in the faith given to you, "which is the mother of us all,"[11] with hope following and charity leading, charity toward God and Christ and our neighbor. For, if a person remain with these, he has fulfilled the commandment of righteousness; for he who has charity is far from all sin.

Now the beginning of all difficulties is the love of money.[12] Since we know then that "we have brought nothing into this world, and can take nothing out of it either,"[13] let us arm ourselves with the armor of righteousness and learn first to advance in the commandment of the Lord. Then let us teach our wives to remain in the faith taught them and in charity and purity to cherish their husbands in all truth, loving all others impartially in complete chastity, and to bring up their children in the fear of God. Teach the widows to be prudent in the faith of the Lord, and to pray without ceasing for all, to keep far from all calumny, slander, false witness, love of money and every evil, knowing that they are an altar of God, that He inspects all things, and that not one of the calculations or thoughts or "the hidden things of the heart"[14] escapes Him.

Knowing, then, that "God is not mocked,"[15] we ought to walk in a manner worthy of His commandment and glory. Similarly, deacons must be blameless in the presence of His justice, like servants of God and Christ, not of men; not slanderers, not double-tongued, not money-lovers, temperate in all things, compassionate, careful, walking according to the truth of the Lord, who became the servant of all.[16] If we be pleasing to Him in this world, we shall receive the future world in accordance with His promises to raise us up from the dead, and, if we act in a manner worthy of Him, "we shall also reign with Him,"[17] provided we believe. The young men, also, must likewise be blameless in all things, cherishing purity above everything else and curbing themselves from every evil.[18] For it is good to be cut off from the lusts in the world, because "all lust wars against the Spirit,"[19] and "neither fornicators nor the effeminate nor sodomites shall inherit the Kingdom of God,"[20] nor those who do unnatural things. Therefore, it is necessary to refrain from all this and to be subject to the presbyters and deacons as to God and Christ. The virgins must walk in a blameless and pure conscience.

And the presbyters also must be sympathetic, merciful to all, guiding back the wanderers,[21] visiting all the sick, neglecting neither widow nor orphan nor pauper, but "always providing what is good before God and men."[22] They must refrain from all anger, from respect of persons, from unfair judgment, and keep far from all love of money; be not quick to believe anything against any man, not hasty in judgment, knowing that we are all under the debt of sin. If, then, we beseech the Lord to forgive us, we should also forgive; for we stand before the eyes of the Lord God, and we "must all stand before the judgment-seat of Christ," and "each must give an account of himself."[23] Accordingly, let us so serve Him with fear and all reverence, as He has commanded and as did the Apostles who evangelized us, and the prophets who foretold of the coming of our Lord; being zealous for what is good, refraining from offenses and false brethren, and from those who carry the name of the Lord in hypocrisy, to mislead foolish men.

"For everyone who does not confess that Jesus Christ has come in the flesh is an antichrist";[24] and whoever does not confess the witness of the

Cross is of the devil; and whoever perverts the sayings of the Lord to his own evil desires and says there is neither resurrection nor judgment, that one is the first-born of Satan. Therefore, let us abandon the vanities of the crowd and their false teachings; let us return to the word which was delivered to us from the beginning. Let us be watchful in prayers[25] and persevere in fasting, beseeching the all-seeing God in petitions "not to lead us into temptation."[26] As the Lord said: "The spirit indeed is willing, but the flesh is weak."[27]

Without interruption, therefore, let us persevere by our hope and by the guarantee of our righteousness,[28] which is Jesus Christ, who "bore our sins in His own body on the tree, who did no sin, nor was deceit found in His mouth";[29] but for our sake, that we might live in Him, He endured all things. Let us, then, become imitators of His patient endurance, and, if we suffer for His name, let us praise Him. For He gave us this example in His own person, and we have believed this.

I exhort you all, then, to obey the word of justice and to practice all endurance as you saw with your own eyes in the blessed Ignatius and Zosimus and Rufus. This you saw also in others from your own group and in Paul himself and the other Apostles. Be convinced that all these "ran not in vain,"[30] but in faith and in righteousness, and that they are with the Lord, with whom they also suffered, in the place which they have deserved. For they "loved not the present world,"[31] but Him who died for them and who was raised up by God for our sakes.

Stand fast, therefore, in this conduct[32] and follow the example of the Lord, "firm and unchangeable in faith, lovers of the brotherhood, loving each other, united in truth,"[33] helping each other with the mildness of the Lord, despising no man.[34] When you can do good,[35] do not put it off, "for almsgiving frees from death."[36] You must all be subject to one another[37] and keep your conduct free from reproach among pagans, so that from your good works[38] you may receive praise and the Lord may not be blasphemed on account of you. But woe to him on whose account the name of the Lord is blasphemed. Teach sobriety, therefore, to all, and practice it yourselves, also.

I have been deeply grieved for Valens, who was once made a presbyter among you, that he so little understands the dignity which was given to him. I warn you, therefore, to abstain from avarice and to be chaste and truthful. Keep away from all evil. If any man cannot control himself in these things, how can he recommend it to another? If a man does not abstain from avarice, he will be defiled by idolatry, and will be judged as one of the pagans, who "know not the judgment of the Lord."[39] Or do we forget "that the saints shall judge the world,"[40] as Paul teaches? However, I have not found nor heard anything of the kind among you, among whom blessed Paul toiled, who were yourselves his epistles[41] in the beginning. For he boasts about you in all the Churches,[42] which alone knew the Lord in those times when we had not yet known Him. I am exceedingly sorry, therefore, for Valens and his wife; may the Lord grant them a true repentance. Therefore, be temperate yourselves in this regard, and do not consider such persons enemies,[43] but invite them back as sinful and erring members, that you may heal the whole body of you. By doing this you edify one another.

I am sure that you are well-trained in the Sacred Scriptures, and that nothing is hid from you, but this is not granted to me. Now, as it is said in these Scriptures: "Be angry and sin not,"[44] and "Let not the sun go down upon your wrath." Blessed is he who remembers this; and I believe that this is so with you. Now, may God and the Father of our Lord Jesus Christ, and the "eternal High-Priest" Himself, Jesus Christ, build you up in faith and truth and in all kindness, free from anger, patient, long-suffering in endurance and chastity. May He give you, too, a share and participation among His saints, and to us along with you, as well as to all under Heaven who shall believe in our Lord and God Jesus Christ and in His Father, who raised Him up from the dead.[45] "Pray for all the saints."[46] "Pray also for the emperors,"[47] and authorities, and rulers, and "for those who persecute and hate you"[48] and for "the enemies of the Cross,"[49] that the result of your effort may be manifest to all men, that you may be perfect in Him.

You wrote to me, both yourselves and Ignatius, that, if anyone was going to Syria, he should also carry letters from you. I will do this if I get a proper opportunity, either myself or the person whom I shall send as a messenger for you also. The letter of Ignatius sent to us by himself and all the others we have here we send you, as you requested; these are subjoined to this epistle, and from them you will greatly profit. For in them there are faith and endurance and all the edification pertaining to our Lord. And let us know whatever you learn concerning Ignatius and those who are with him.

I have written this to you by Crescens, whom I recommended to you recently and whom I again commend. For he has behaved blamelessly among us, and I believe likewise among you. You will receive a recommendation of his sister, also, when she shall come to you. Farewell. Good-bye to you in the Lord Jesus Christ in grace, and to all who are with you. Amen.

Questions for Polycarp

1. What does Polycarp say about the characteristics of righteousness?
2. Describe the qualities of a good priest (presbyter).
3. In what way did the priest Valens go wrong?

Notes

1. Acts 2:24.
2. 1 Pet. 1:8.
3. Eph. 2:8.
4. 1 Pet. 1:3.
5. 1 Pet. 1:21.
6. Acts 10:42.
7. 2 Cor. 4:14.
8. 1 Pet. 3:9.
9. Matt. 7:1–2; Luke 6:36–38.
10. Matt. 5:3,10.
11. Gal. 4:26.
12. Cf. 1 Tim. 6:10.
13. Cf. 1 Tim. 6:7.
14. 1 Cor. 14:25.
15. Gal. 6:7.
16. Mark 9:33.
17. 2 Tim. 2:12.
18. 1 Pet. 2:11.
19. Gal. 5:17.
20. 1 Cor. 6:9–10.
21. Ezek. 34:4.
22. 2 Cor. 8:21.
23. Rom. 14:10,12.
24. 1 John 4:2–3.
25. 1 Pet. 4:7.

26. Matt. 6:13.
27. Matt. 26:41.
28. Mark 14:38.
29. 1 Pet. 2:22,24.
30. Phil. 2:16.
31. 1 Tim. 4:10.
32. 1 Cor. 15:58.
33. 1 Pet. 2:17.
34. Rom. 12:10.
35. Prov. 3:28.
36. Tob. 4:11.
37. Eph. 5:21.
38. 1 Pet. 2:12.
39. Jer. 5:4.
40. 1 Cor. 6:2.
41. 2 Cor. 3:2.
42. 1 Thess. 1:4.
43. 2 Thess. 3:15.
44. Ps. 4:5.
45. Gal. 1:1.
46. Eph. 6:18.
47. 1 Tim. 2:1.
48. Matt. 5:44.
49. Phil. 3:18.

St. John Chrysostom

St. John Chrysostom (A.D. 347–407), who received the name
"Chrysostom" (golden mouth) for his eloquence as a preacher, au-
thored this treatise in the 380s. The six "books," which today would
be called chapters, form a unified whole in which Chrysostom discusses his own vocation to the priesthood and the responsibilities
that belong to it. It bears the influence of an earlier short treatise on
the priesthood, St. Gregory of Nazianzus's De Fuga (A.D. 362). The
book is written as a dialogue between John and his friend Basil,
whose identity is unknown. In the excerpt, from the beginning of
Book III, Chrysostom emphasizes that a priest or bishop must be
free from all worldly ambition. He shows that a priest or bishop's
public role will make worldly honors a severe temptation for him.

THERE ARE MANY OTHER QUALITIES, Basil, in addition to those I have
mentioned, which a priest ought to have, and which I lack. And the
first of all is that he must purify his soul entirely of ambition for the office. For if he is strongly attracted to this office, when he gets it he will
add fuel to the fire and, being mastered by ambition, he will tolerate all
kinds of evil to secure his hold upon it, even resorting to flattery, or sub-
mitting to mean and unworthy treatment, or spending lavishly. I pass

From: Six Books on the Priesthood, Book III, trans. Graham Neville, chap. 10–14
(Crestwood, N.Y.: St. Vladimir's Seminary Press, 1996), 80–88. Used by permission of St. Vladimir's Seminary Press, 575 Scarsdale Road, Crestwood, N.Y.,
10707, (800) 204-2665.

over for the moment, for fear of seeming to say things beyond credit, the fact that some men, in contending for this office, have filled the churches with murder and split cities into factions.

The right course, I think, is to have so reverent an estimation of the office as to avoid its responsibility from the start; and, after being appointed to it, not to wait for the judgment of others, if you should happen to have committed a sin that calls for deposition, but to anticipate this and depose yourself from office. In this way a man will probably induce God's mercy. But if he clings to a position for which he is not fit, he deprives himself of all pardon and provokes God's anger the more by adding a second and more serious offence. But no one will ever be content to do so; for it is indeed a terrible temptation to covet this honor. And in saying this, I do not contradict St. Paul, but entirely agree with what he says. What are his words? "If a man seeks the office of a bishop, he desires a good work."[1] I meant it was terrible to desire, not the work, but the absolute authority and power.

I think a man must rid his mind of this ambition with all possible care, and not for a moment let it be governed by it, in order that he may always act with freedom. For if he does not want to achieve fame in this position of authority, he will not dread its loss either. And if he does not fear this, he can always act with the freedom which befits Christian men. But those who fear and dread deposition from this office endure a bitter slavery, full of all kinds of evil, and cannot help often offending man and God.

But the soul ought not to be in this condition. As in war we see soldiers of fine spirit fighting eagerly and falling bravely, so those who have come to this administration should be ready either to be consecrated to the office or to be relieved of it, as befits Christian men, knowing that such deposition earns a crown no less than the office itself.

For when anyone has this done to him because he will not submit to anything which is unbecoming or unworthy of his position, he procures a greater punishment for those who wrongfully depose him, and a greater reward for himself. "Blessed are you," says our Lord, "when men shall reproach you and persecute you, and say all manner of evil against you falsely for my sake. Rejoice and be exceeding glad; for great is your reward in heaven."[2] This is surely true even when anyone is expelled by men of his own order, either through envy or to please others or through enmity or any other wrong motive. But when he gets his treatment from his enemies, I do not think any argument is needed to prove how great a benefit they confer on him by their wickedness.

So we must be thoroughly on our guard against ambition and examine ourselves carefully to prevent a spark of it from smouldering anywhere unseen. It is much to be desired that those who at first were free from this infection should be able to keep clear of it when they have entered office. But if anyone nurtures within himself this terrible, savage beast before attaining office, there is no telling what a furnace he will fling himself into, after he has attained it. For my own part (and do not think that I would ever lie to you out of self-depreciation), I possess this ambition in a high degree. And this fact, quite as much as all the other reasons, alarmed me and impelled me to run away as I did. For just as lovers of a human person endure a terrible torment of passion as long as they can be near the objects of their love, but throw off their frenzy when they take themselves as far away as possible from those whom they desire; so also those who covet this office find the evil intolerable while they are near it, but quench the desire along with the expectation, as soon as they give up hope.

This, then, was one strong motive, and even if it had been all by itself, it would have been enough to debar me from this dignity. In fact, however, there is another motive quite as strong. What is it? A priest must be sober and clear-sighted and possess a thousand eyes looking in every direction, for he lives, not for himself alone, but for a great multitude. But I am sluggish and remiss and scarcely sufficient for my own salvation, as even you should admit, though you are most of all eager to hide my faults for love's sake.

Do not speak to me now of fasting and vigils and sleeping on the ground and other bodily discipline. You know how far short I come even in these. But if these exercises had been most carefully regulated by me, they would have been unable to equip me at all for this responsibility, while my sluggishness remained. They would be a great help to someone shut up in a cell and concerned only about his own soul. But when a man is distracted by such a huge multitude and inherits all the private cares of those who are under his rule, what appreciable help can these practices continue towards their improvement, unless he has a healthy, robust soul?

Do not be surprised if, in addition to such endurance, I apply another touchstone of spiritual strength. We can see that contempt for food and drink and soft bedding comes easily to many, especially to more uncouth natures brought up in that way from early childhood, but to many others as well. For bodily constitution and practice mitigate the severity of those exercises. But there are not many, indeed only one or two here and there, who can bear insult and abuse and vulgar language and taunts from inferiors, spoken casually or deliberately, and complaints made at random by the rulers and the ruled. You see men who are valiant in ascetic practices so far losing their heads at these that they become wilder than savage beasts. We must debar such men in particular from the precincts of the priesthood. For it would not harm the common life of the Church if a prelate should neither starve himself of food, nor go barefoot. But a furious temper causes great disasters both to its possessor and to his neighbors. There is no threat from God against those who omit these ascetic practices, but those who are angry without a cause are threatened with hell and hell fire.[3] As, then, the lover of vainglory adds fresh fuel to the fire when he assumes the government of numbers, so a man who cannot control his temper while alone or in the company of a few others, but is easily thrown into a passion, is like a wild beast baited by crowds all around, when he is entrusted with the rule of an entire congregation. He cannot live at peace himself and spreads evils galore among the people committed to his charge.

Nothing muddies the purity of the mind and the perspicacity of the wits as much as an ungovernable temper that fluctuates violently. Scripture says, "This destroys even the prudent."[4] For the soul's eye is darkened, as in a night battle, and cannot distinguish friend from foe or worthless from worthy. It treats all in turn alike (even though some evil consequence ensues), carelessly accepting every consequence to gratify the soul's pleasure, even if it means a crop of trouble. For a blazing temper is a kind of pleasure, and it tyrannizes over the soul more harshly than pleasure, thoroughly upsetting all its healthy condition. It easily excites men to insolence, to ill-timed enmities and unreasonable hatred, and is forever making them give willful offence and forcing them to say and do many other things just as bad. For the soul is swept along with the strong rush of passion and has no base on which to rest its own strength and resist so strong an attack.

Basil: I will not put up with your humbug any longer. Who knows better than I how free you are from this disease?

John: Why, then, my dear fellow, do you want to drag me near the pyre and bait the sleeping beast? Do you not know that my freedom from this fault is due, not to my innate goodness, but to my love of retirement? It is good for anyone in this condition (not to mention anyone who has fallen into the very abyss of heavy anxieties) to remain by himself or keep company with one or two friends, and so manage to avoid being set on fire with this passion. For otherwise he drags, not himself only, but many others with him, to the brink of ruin, and makes them more careless about the cultivation of a gentle character. For the mass of people under government are, for the most part, prone to regard the character of their rulers as a kind of archetype, and to assimilate themselves to it. And how can anyone stop their outbursts, if he is excitable himself? What ordinary man would naturally want to learn self-control when he sees his ruler is hot-tempered?

The priest's shortcomings simply cannot be concealed. On the contrary, even the most trivial soon get known. The weakest athlete can keep his weakness secret as long as he remains at home and pits himself against nobody; but when he strips for the contest, he is soon shown up. So with other men: those who lead a retired and inactive life have their solitude as a cloak for their private faults; but when they are brought into public life, they are compelled to strip off their retirement like a garment and to show everyone their naked souls by their outward movements. As, then, their right actions benefit many and challenge them to equal efforts, so their faults make other men careless in the quest of virtue, and encourage them to shirk hard work for the things that matter. Therefore the beauty of his soul must shine out brightly all round, to be able to gladden and enlighten the souls of those who see.

The sins of ordinary men are committed in the dark, so to speak, and ruin only those who commit them. But when a man becomes famous and is known to many, his misdeeds inflict a common injury on all. They make backsliders even more supine in their efforts for what is good, and drive to despair those who want to improve. Apart from this, the offences of the insignificant, even if made public, harm no one seriously. But those who are set upon the pinnacle of this honor not only catch every eye; more than that, however trifling their offences, these little things seem great to others, since everyone measures sin, not by the size of the offence, but by the standing of the sinner.

The priest must be armed with weapons of steel—intense earnestness and constant sobriety of life—and he must keep watch in every direction, in case anyone should find a naked and unguarded spot and strike him a mortal blow. For everyone stands round him ready to wound him and strike him down, not only his enemies and foes, but many of those who pretend to love him. We must, therefore, choose souls as hardy as God's grace once proved the bodies of the saints in the Babylonian furnace.[5] The fuel of this fire is not brushwood, pitch, and tow, but something far worse than that. It is no material fire to which they are exposed, but the all-devouring flame of malice envelops them, rising up all round, and attacking them and searching their life more thoroughly than the fire did the bodies of those young men. When it finds the slightest trace of stubble, it quickly lays hold of it and burns up the rotten part, while all the rest of the building, even though brighter than rays of sunshine, is scorched and blackened completely by the smoke.

For as long as the priest's life is well regulated in every particular point, their intrigues cannot hurt him. But if he should overlook some small detail, as is likely for a human being on his journey across the devious ocean of his life, all the rest of his good deeds are of no avail to enable him to escape the words of his accusers. That small offence casts a shadow over all the rest of his life. Everyone wants to judge the priest, not as one clothed in flesh, not as one possessing a human nature, but as an angel, exempt from the frailty of others.

Everyone fears and flatters a tyrant as long as his power lasts, because they cannot depose him. But when they see his power decline, those who were just now his friends throw off their hypocritical esteem and suddenly become his foes and enemies. When they have discovered all his weaknesses, they set upon him and depose him from power. So it is with priests. Those who but now flattered and courted him when he was in power, once they have found the least handle, eagerly make plans to depose him, not merely as a tyrant, but as something far worse than that. Again, as a tyrant fears his bodyguard, so he dreads above all his neighbors and fellow ministers. For other people do not covet a tyrant's power as much, nor, above all, know his business as well, as these men know his. Being close to him, they learn before others of any faults that may occur. If they slander him, they can easily gain credence, and if they exaggerate trifles, they can convict the victim of their pettifogging. For the well-known saying of the Apostle has been inverted: "And if one member suffers, all the members rejoice; and if one member is honored, all the members suffer,"[6] unless by great discretion someone can survive it all.

Are you, then, sending me forth to such a terrible war? Did you judge my spirit adequate for so complex and intricate a battle? Where did you get the information? And from whom? If it was God who revealed it, show me the oracle, and I will obey. But if you cannot do so and are making a judgment from human opinion, then deceive yourself no longer. For you should believe me rather than others about myself, since "no man knows the things of a man, save the spirit of the man which is in him."[7]

With these arguments I think I must have persuaded you now, if not before, that I should have made both myself and those who chose me ridiculous by accepting this office, and that I should have returned again to the path of life in which I now am, but at great cost. For it is not only malice, but something far worse than malice—ambition for office—that usually arms the majority of men against the one who possesses it. And as covetous sons begrudge their fathers a long life, so when some of these men see the priestly office held by anyone for a prolonged period, they are anxious to depose him, as it would hardly be right to murder him! For they are all ambitious to succeed him and everyone expects that the office will fall to himself.

Questions for John Chrysostom

1. What problems are caused by ambition and ungovernable temper?
2. What attributes of spiritual strength does John think a good priest or bishop must have?
3. How does John describe the pressures and difficulties of being a priest or bishop? What are the dangers and temptations of public office, even for a good priest or bishop?

Notes

1. 1 Tim. 3:1.
2. Matt. 5:11–12.

3. Cf. Matt. 5:22.
4. Prov. 15:1 (LXX).
5. Dan. 3:27.
6. Cf. 1 Cor. 12:26.
7. Cf. I Cor. 2:11.

St. Ambrose

St. Ambrose (A.D. 340–397), bishop of Milan from 374 until his death, baptized St. Augustine and wrote numerous treatises on Christian faith and practice. He composed his treatise on the priesthood, from which the following excerpt is taken, around 391. Seeking to inculcate virtue among the clergy, he based his treatise on the great Roman moralist Cicero's *De Officiis*. St. Ambrose's treatise is filled with practical advice to priests and bishops on how to lead virtuous lives befitting their office. In the following excerpt, he warns particularly against the love of money.

I THINK, THEN, THAT ONE should strive to win preferment, especially in the Church, only by good actions and with a right aim; so that there may be no proud conceit, no idle carelessness, no shameful disposition of mind, no unseemly ambition. A plain simplicity of mind is enough for everything, and commends itself quite sufficiently.

When in office, again, it is not right to be harsh and severe, nor may one be too easy; lest on the one hand we should seem to be exercising a despotic power, and on the other to be by no means filling the office we had taken up.

From: Duties of the Clergy, Book II, trans. H. de Romestin, Nicene and Post-Nicene Fathers Series, ed. Philip Schaff, vol. 10: Ambrose: Select Works and Letters (Peabody, Mass.: Hendrickson, 1994), 61–65.

We must strive also to win many by kindnesses and duties that we can do, and to preserve the favor already shown us. For they will with good reason forget the benefits of former times if they are now vexed at some great wrong. For it often enough happens that those one has shown favor to and allowed to rise step by step, are driven away, if one decides in some unworthy way to put another before them. But it is seemly for a priest to show such favor in his kindnesses and his decisions as to guard equity, and to show regard to the other clergy as to parents.

Those who once stood approved should not now become overbearing, but rather, as mindful of the grace that they have received, stand firm in their humility. A priest ought not to be offended if either cleric or attendant or any ecclesiastic should win regard for himself, by showing mercy, or by fasting, or by uprightness of life, or by teaching and reading. For the grace of the Church is the praise of the teacher. It is a good thing that the work of another should be praised, if only it be done without any desire to boast. For each one should receive praise from the lips of his neighbor, and not from his own mouth, and each one should be commended by the work he has done, not merely by the wishes he had.

But if any one is disobedient to his bishop and wishes to exalt and upraise himself, and to overshadow his bishop's merits by a feigned appearance of learning or humility or mercy, he is wandering from the truth in his pride; for the rule of truth is, to do nothing to advance one's own cause whereby another loses ground, nor to use whatever good one has to the disgrace or blame of another.

Never protect a wicked man, nor allow the sacred things to be given over to an unworthy one; on the other hand, do not harass and press hard on a man whose fault is not clearly proved. Injustice quickly gives offence in every case, but especially in the Church, where equity ought to exist, where like treatment should be given to all, so that a powerful person may not claim the more, nor a rich man appropriate the more. For whether we be poor or rich, we are one in Christ. Let him that lives a holier life claim nothing more thereby for himself; for he ought rather to be the more humble for it.

In giving judgment let us have no respect of persons. Favor must be put out of sight, and the case be decided on its merits. Nothing is so great a strain on another's good opinion or confidence, as the fact of our giving away the cause of the weaker to the more powerful in any case that comes before us. The same happens if we are hard on the poor, while we make excuses for the rich man when guilty. Men are ready enough to flatter those in high positions, so as not to let them think themselves injured, or to feel vexed as though overthrown. But if you fear to give offence then do not undertake to give judgment. If you are a priest or some cleric do not urge it. It is allowable for you to be silent in the matter, if it be a money affair, though it is always due to consistency to be on the side of equity. But in the cause of God, where there is danger to the whole Church, it is no small sin to act as though one saw nothing.

But what advantage is it to you to show favor to a rich man? Is it that he is more ready to repay one who loves him? For we generally show favor to those from whom we expect to receive a return of favor. But we ought to think far more of the weak and helpless, because we hope to receive, on behalf of him who has it not, a recompense from the Lord Jesus, Who in the likeness of a marriage feast[1] has given us a general representation of virtue. By this He bids us confer benefits rather on those who cannot give them to us in return, teaching us to bid to our feasts and meals, not those who are rich, but those that are poor. For the rich seem to be asked that they may prepare a banquet for us in return; the poor, as they have nothing wherewith to make return, when they receive anything, make the Lord to be our recompense Who has offered Himself as surety for the poor.

In the ordinary course of things, too, the conferring of a benefit on the poor is of more use than when it is conferred on the rich. The rich man scorns the benefit and is ashamed to feel indebted for a favor. Nay, moreover, whatever is offered to him he takes as due to his merits, as though only a just debt were paid him; or else he thinks it was but given because the giver expected a still greater return to be made him by the rich man. So, in accepting a kindness, the rich man, on that very ground, thinks that he has given more than he ever received. The poor man, however, though he has no money wherewith he can repay, at least shows his gratitude. And herein it is certain that he returns more than he received. For money is paid in coins, but gratitude never fails; money grows less by payment, but gratitude fails when held back, and is preserved when given to others. Next—a thing the rich man avoids—the poor man owns that he feels bound by the debt. He really thinks help has been given him, not that it has been offered in return for his honor.

He considers that his children have been again given him, that his life is restored and his family preserved. How much better, then, is it to confer benefits upon the good than on the ungrateful.

Wherefore the Lord said to His disciples: "Take neither gold nor silver nor money."[2] Whereby as with a sickle He cuts off the love of money that is ever growing up in human hearts. Peter also said to the lame man, who was always carried even from his mother's womb: "Silver and gold have I none, but what I have I give you. In the Name of Jesus Christ of Nazareth, arise and walk."[3] So he gave not money, but he gave health. How much better it is to have health without money, than money without health! The lame man rose; he had not hoped for that: he received no money; though he had hoped for that. But riches are hardly to be found among the saints of the Lord, so as to become objects of contempt to them.

But man's habits have so long applied themselves to this admiration of money, that no one is thought worthy of honor unless he is rich. This is no new habit. Nay, this vice (and that makes the matter worse) grew long years ago in the hearts of men. When the city of Jericho fell at the sound of the priests' trumpets and Joshua the son of Nun gained the victory, he knew that the valor of the people was weakened through love of money and desire for gold. For when Achan had taken a garment of gold and two hundred shekels of silver and a golden ingot from the spoils of the ruined city, he was brought before the Lord, and could not deny the theft, but owned it.[4]

Love of money, then, is an old, an ancient vice, which showed itself even at the declaration of the divine law; for a law was given to check it.[5] On account of love of money Balak thought Balaam could be tempted by rewards to curse the people of our fathers.[6] Love of money would have won the day, too, had not God bidden him hold back from cursing. Overcome by love of money Achan led to destruction all the people of the fathers. So Joshua the son of Nun, who could stay the sun from setting, could not stay the love of money in man from creeping on. At the sound of his voice the sun stood still, but love of money stayed not. When the sun stood still Joshua completed his triumph, but when love of money went on, he almost lost the victory.

Why? Did not the woman Delilah's love of money deceive Samson, the bravest man of all?[7] So he who had torn asunder the roaring lion with his hands;[8] who, when bound and handed over to his enemies, alone, without help, burst his bonds and slew a thousand of them;[9] who broke the cords interwoven with sinews as though they were but the slight threads of a net; he, I say, having laid his head on the woman's knee, was robbed of the decoration of his victory-bringing hair, that which gave him his might. Money flowed into the lap of the woman, and the favor of God forsook the man.[10]

Love of money, then, is deadly. Seductive is money, whilst it also defiles those who have it, and helps not those who have it not. Supposing that money sometimes is a help, yet it is only a help to a poor man who makes his want known. What good is it to him who does not long for it, nor seek it; who does not need its help and is not turned aside by pursuit of it? What good is it to others, if he who has it is alone the richer for it? Is he therefore more honorable because he has that whereby honor is often lost, because he has what he must guard rather than possess? We possess what we use, but what is beyond our use brings us no fruit of possession, but only the danger of watching.

To come to an end; we know that contempt of riches is a form of justice, therefore we ought to avoid love of money, and strive with all our powers never to do anything against justice, but to guard it in all our deeds and actions.

If we would please God, we must have love, we must be of one mind, we must follow humility, each one thinking the other higher than himself. This is true humility, when one never claims anything proudly for oneself, but thinks oneself to be the inferior. The bishop should treat the clerics and attendants, who are indeed his sons, as members of himself, and give to each one that duty for which he sees him to be fit.

Not without pain is a limb of the body cut off which has become corrupt. It is treated for a long time, to see if it can be cured with various remedies. If it cannot be cured, then it is cut off by a good physician. Thus it is a good bishop's desire to wish to heal the weak, to remove the spreading ulcers, to burn some parts and not to cut them off; and lastly, when they cannot be healed, to cut them off with pain to himself. Wherefore that beautiful rule of the Apostle stands forth brightly, that we should look each one, not on his own things, but on the things of others.[11] In this way it will never come about that we shall in anger give way to our own feelings, or concede more than is right in favor to our own wishes.

It is a very great incentive to mercy to share in others' misfortunes, to help the needs of others as far as our means allow, and sometimes even beyond them. For it is better for mercy's sake to take up a case, or to suffer odium rather than to show hard feeling. So I once brought odium on myself because I broke up the sacred vessels to redeem captives—a fact that could displease the Arians. Not that it displeased them as an act, but as being a thing in which they could take hold of something for which to blame me. Who can be so hard, cruel, iron-hearted, as to be displeased because a man is redeemed from death, or a woman from barbarian impurities, things that are worse than death, or boys and girls and infants from the pollution of idols, whereby through fear of death they were defiled?

Although we did not act thus without good reason, yet we have followed it up among the people so as to confess and to add again and again that it was far better to preserve souls than gold for the Lord. For He Who sent the apostles without gold[12] also brought together the churches without gold. The Church has gold, not to store up, but to lay out, and to spend on those who need. What necessity is there to guard what is of no good? Do we not know how much gold and silver the Assyrians took out of the temple of the Lord?[13] Is it not much better that the priests should melt it down for the sustenance of the poor, if other supplies fail, than that a sacrilegious enemy should carry it off and defile it? Would not the Lord Himself say: Why did you suffer so many needy to die of hunger? Surely you had gold? You should have given them sustenance. Why are so many captives brought on the slave market, and why are so many unredeemed left to be slain by the enemy? It had been better to preserve living vessels than gold ones.

To this no answer could be given. For what would you say: I feared that the temple of God would need its ornaments? He would answer: The sacraments need not gold, nor are they proper to gold only—for they are not bought with gold. The glory of the sacraments is the redemption of captives. Truly they are precious vessels, for they redeem men from death. That, indeed, is the true treasure of the Lord which effects what His blood effected. Then, indeed, is the vessel of the Lord's blood recognized, when one sees in either redemption, so that the chalice redeems from the enemy those whom His blood redeemed from sin. How beautifully it is said, when long lines of captives are redeemed by the Church: These Christ has redeemed. Behold the gold that can be tried, behold the useful gold, behold the gold of Christ which frees from death, behold the gold whereby modesty is redeemed and chastity is preserved.

Questions for Ambrose

1. What is "the rule of truth" as set forth by Ambrose?
2. Why does Ambrose warn so strongly against the temptation of priests and bishops to show favor to the rich?
3. Why must the Church strive not to be infected with the "love of money"? What is the Church's true treasure?

Notes

1. Lk 14:12,13.
2. Mt 10:9.
3. Acts 3:6.
4. Josh. 7:21.
5. Ex 20:17.
6. Num. 22:17.
7. Judg. 16:6.
8. Judg. 14:6.
9. Judg. 15:14,15.
10. Judg. 16:20.
11. Phil. 2:4.
12. Mt 10:9.
13. 2 Kings 24:13.

St. Gregory the Great

St. Gregory the Great (A.D. 540–604) was abbot of St. Andrew's
Monastery in Rome when he was elected Pope in 590. Soon after his
election, he composed *Pastoral Care* (or, as it is also known, the *Book
of Pastoral Rule*), which sets forth the responsibilities of the pastoral
office and offers advice on how the priest or bishop should fulfill
these duties. The book has four parts, the first addressing the duties
of the pastor, the second the inner and outer life of a faithful pastor,
the third how the pastor should teach and govern, and the fourth the
need for humility. Indebted to the works of the earlier Fathers, especially St. Gregory of Nazianzus, *Pastoral Care* provides valuable reflections on how the pastor should govern his flock. The following
excerpt emphasizes that a truly humble priest or bishop will not be
a weak leader.

THE RULER SHOULD IN humility be the comrade of those who lead good
lives but stern with the vices of evildoers. He must not set himself
over the good in any way, and when the sins of the wicked demand it, he
must assert the power of his supremacy at once. Thus, waiving aside his
rank, he regards himself the equal of his subjects who lead good lives,
but does not shrink from exercising the laws of rectitude against the perverse. For, as I remember to have said in the *Books on Morals*,[1] it is clear

Excerpts from *Pastoral Care*, trans. by Henry Davis, S. J., Ancient Christian Writ-
ers Series, ed. Johannes Quasten, vol. 2, copyright © 1950, 59–67. Used with Permission of Paulist Press, *www.paulistpress.com*.

that nature brought forth all men in equality, while guilt has placed some below others, in accordance with the order of their varying demerits. This diversity, which results from vice, is a dispensation of the divine judgment, much as one man must be ruled by another, since all men cannot be on equal footing.

Wherefore, all who are superiors should not regard in themselves the power of their rank, but the equality of their nature; and they should find their joy not in ruling over men, but in helping them. For our ancient fathers are recorded to have been not kings of men, but shepherds of flocks. And when the Lord said to Noah and his sons: "Increase and multiply and fill the earth," He at once added: "And let the fear and dread of you be upon all the beasts of the earth."[2] Fear and dread were prescribed for all the beasts of the earth, but forbidden to be exercised over men. By nature a man is made superior to the beasts, but not to other men; it is, therefore, said to him that he is to be feared by beasts, but not by men. Evidently, to wish to be feared by an equal is to lord it over others, contrary to the natural order.

Yet it is necessary that rulers should be feared by subjects, when they see that the latter do not fear God. Lacking fear of God's judgments, these must at least fear sin out of human respect. It is not at all a case of exhibiting pride when superiors seek to inspire fear, whereby they do not seek personal glory, but the righteousness of their subjects. In fact, in inspiring fear in those who lead evil lives, superiors lord it, as it were, over beasts, not over men, because insofar as their subjects are beasts, they ought also to be subjugated by fear.

Often, however, a ruler by the very fact of his preeminence over others becomes conceited; and because everything is at his service, because his orders are quickly executed to suit his wishes, because all his subjects praise him for what he has done well but have no authority to criticize what he has done amiss and because they usually praise even what they ought to blame, his mind, led astray by those below him, is lifted above itself. While he is outwardly surrounded by abounding favors, the truth within him is made void. Forgetful of what he is, he is diverted by the commendations of others, and believes himself to be such as he hears himself outwardly proclaimed to be, not such as he should inwardly judge himself. He despises his subjects and does not acknowledge them to be his equals in the order of nature; and those whom he has excelled by the fortuity of power, he believes he has also surpassed by the merits of his life. He esteems himself to be wiser than any of those whom he sees he exceeds in power. For he puts himself on an eminence in his own estimation, and though he has his own limitations by reason of the equality of nature with others, he disdains to regard others as being on his level. He thus brings himself to be the like of him of whom Scripture says: "He beholds every high thing, and he is king over all the children of pride."[3] He who aspired to singular eminence and disdained life in common with the angels, said: "I will place my seat in the North, I will be like the Most High."[4] By a wonderful decree, therefore, he finds within himself the pit of his downfall, while outwardly exalting himself on the pinnacle of power. Man is made like the apostate angel when he disdains, though a man, to be like other men.

In this way Saul, after having distinguished himself for his humility, was swollen with pride in the eminence of his power; by his humility he was advanced, by his pride, rejected, as the Lord attested, saying: "When you were a little one in thy own eyes, did I not make you the head of the tribes of Israel?"[5] He had previously seen himself a little one in his own eyes, but relying on temporal power, he no longer saw himself to be the little one. Preferring himself to others, he regarded himself great above all others, because he had greater power than they. And in a wonderful way, while a little one in his own esteem, he was great with God, but when he thought himself to be great, he was little with God.

Usually, then, when the mind of a man is inflated with a multitude of subjects under him, he becomes corrupted and moved to pride by the eminence of his power which panders to the mind. But such power is truly well-controlled by one who knows how both to assert and oppose it. He controls it well who knows how through it to obtain the mastery over sin, and knows how with it to associate with others on terms of equality. For the human mind is prone to pride even when not supported by power; how much more, then, does it exalt itself when it has that support! But he disposes his power aright, who knows how, with great care, both to derive from it what is profitable, and to subdue the temptations which it creates, and how, though in possession of it, to realize his equality with others, and at the same time set himself above sinners in his zeal for retribution.

This is a distinction which will be more fully understood when we consider the examples given by the first Pastor. Peter, who held from God the primacy in Holy Church, refused to accept excessive veneration from Cornelius though he acted rightly in humbly prostrating himself; but Peter acknowledged in him his equal when he said: "Arise, do not act so; I myself also am a man."[6] But when the guilt of Ananias and Sapphira were discovered by him, he at once showed with what great authority he had been made preeminent over others.[7] By his word he smote their life when he laid it bare by his penetrating spirit. He recalled to his mind that in the question of opposition to sin he was supreme in the Church, but such distinction was not present to his mind when among upright brethren honor was eagerly exhibited to him. In the one instance holy conduct was met by the assertion of common equality; in the other, zeal for retributive justice revealed the right of authority.

Paul showed no consciousness of his preeminence over his deserving brethren when he said: "Not because we exercise dominion over your faith, but we are helpers of your joy"; and he presently added: "For in faith you stand,"[8] as if to explain what he had said, namely: "We do not lord it over your faith, for in faith you stand, and we are equals with you wherein we know you stand." It was as if he was not aware of his preeminence over his brethren when he said: "We became little ones in the midst of you";[9] and again: ". . . and ourselves your servants through Christ."[10] But when he discovered a fault which required correction, he at once remembered that he was master, saying: "What will you? Shall I come to you with a rod?"[11]

Supreme rank is, therefore, well-administered, when the superior lords it over vices rather than over brethren. When rulers correct their delinquent subjects, it is incumbent on them to observe carefully that, while they smite faults with due discipline in virtue of their authority, they acknowledge, by observing humility, that they are only the equals of the brethren whom they correct. But we should as a regular practice in thoughtful silence prefer to ourselves those whom we correct, for it is through us that their vices are smitten with rigorous discipline, whereas in the case of our own vices we are not chastised even by verbal censure of anyone. Therefore, we are the more bound before the Lord, inasmuch as we sin with impunity before men. On the other hand, our discipline renders our subjects the more exempt from the divine judgment, as it does not exempt them here from punishment for their faults.

Consequently, humility must be preserved in the heart, and discipline in action. Between these two, we must diligently beware not to relax the rights of government by immoderate adherence to the virtue of humility, for if the superior depreciates himself unduly, he may be unable to restrain the lives of subjects under the bond of discipline. Let rulers, therefore, uphold externally what they undertake for the service of others, and internally retain their fear in their estimate of themselves. Nevertheless, let the subjects themselves perceive, by signs becomingly manifested, that their rulers are humble in their own estimation. They should thus apprehend both what they ought to fear from authority, and what to imitate in the sphere of humility.

Superiors, then, should ceaselessly take care that the greater the external manifestation of power, the more is it to be kept in subjection internally. It must not subdue their thought, it must not so carry the mind away as to captivate it for itself; otherwise the mind will be unable to control that to which it subjects itself in its lust for domination. That the mind of the ruler may not be carried away and elated in the enjoyment of power, it is rightly said by a man of wisdom: "Have they made you a ruler? Be not lifted up, but be among them as one of them."[12] So, too, Peter says: ". . . not as lording it over the clergy, but being made a pattern of the flock."[13] So, the Truth in person, inviting us to the more sublime merits of virtue, says: "You know that the princes of the Gentiles lord it over them, and they that are the greater exercise power upon them. It shall not be so among you, but whosoever will be the greater among you, let him be your minister; and he that will be first among you, shall be your servant. Even as the Son of man is not come to be ministered unto, but to minister."[14]

Wherefore it is that He indicates the punishment in store for the servant who becomes proud on his assumption of rule, saying: "But if that evil servant shall say in his heart: My lord is long in coming, and shall begin to strike his fellow servants, and shall eat and drink with drunkards, the lord of that servant shall come in a day that he hopes not, and at an hour that he knows not; and shall separate him, and appoint his portion with the hypocrites."[15] That man is rightly accounted a hypocrite, who diverts the ministry of government to purposes of domination.

Sometimes, though, greater evil ensues when in the case of wicked persons a policy of equality is adhered to rather than of discipline. Heli, for example, overcome by misguided affection, and unwilling to chastise his delinquent sons, struck both himself and his sons before the strict Judge with a cruel sentence, for the divine utterance was: "You have honored you sons rather than me."[16] So, too, he chides the shepherds by the

Prophet, saying: "That which was broken you have not bound up, and that which was driven away you have not brought back."[17] One who has been cast away is brought back when, after having fallen into sin, he is recalled to the state of righteousness by the influence of pastoral care; for the ligature binds a fracture when discipline subdues sin, lest the wound's continued flow lead to death if a tight compress does not bind it up. Often, however, the fracture is made worse by an unskillful ligature, so that the lesion causes even greater pain from being bound up too tightly.

Wherefore, it is necessary that when the wound of sin in the subject is repressed by correction, even the restraint must be most carefully moderated, lest the feeling of kindness be extinguished by the manner in which the principles of discipline are exercised against the sinner. For care must be taken that loving-kindness, like that of a mother, be displayed by the ruler towards his subject, and correction given as by a father. In all such cases treatment must be bestowed with care and circumspection, lest discipline be too rigid, or loving-kindness too lax.

We have said in the *Books on Morals* that either discipline or compassion is greatly wanting if one is exercised independently of the other.[18] But rulers in their relations with subjects should be animated by compassion duly considerate and by discipline affectionately severe. This is what the Truth teaches[19] concerning the man who was half-dead and was taken to an inn by the care of a Samaritan, wine and oil being applied to his wounds, the wine to cauterize them, and the oil to soothe them. Thus it is necessary that he who sees to the healing of the wounds should apply in wine biting pain and in oil soothing tenderness, for wine cleanses suppuration and oil promotes the course of healing. In other words, gentleness is to be mingled with severity; a compound is to be made of both, so that subjects may not be exasperated by too much great harshness, nor enervated by excessive tenderness.

This, as St. Paul says,[20] is well symbolized by that Ark of the Tabernacle, in which, together with the Tables, were the rod and the manna; because if with the knowledge of the Sacred Scriptures in the breast of the good ruler there is the restraining rod, there should also be the manna of sweetness. Wherefore, David says: "Thy rod and Thy staff, they have comforted me."[21] It is with a rod that we are smitten, but we are supported by a staff. If, then, there is the correction of the rod in striking, let there be the comfort of the staff in supporting.

There should, then, be love that does not enervate, vigor that does not exasperate, zeal not too immoderate and uncontrolled, loving-kindness that spares, yet not more than is befitting. Thus, while justice and clemency are blended in supreme rule, the ruler will soothe the hearts of his subjects even when he inspires fear, and yet in soothing them, hold them to reverential awe for him.

Questions for Gregory the Great

1. How does Gregory try to ensure that power does not corrupt the clergy (priests, bishops, Pope)? In what cases should the authority of the priesthood be exercised?
2. How does Peter, according to Gregory, exemplify the proper use of priestly authority? Why is discipline necessary?

Notes

1. *Mor.* 21. 15:22.
2. Gen. 9:1 f.
3. Job 41:25.
4. Cf. Isa. 14:13 f.
5. 1 Kings 15:17.
6. Acts 10:26.
7. Cf. Acts 5:3–5.
8. 2 Cor. 1:23.
9. 1 Thess. 2:7.
10. 2 Cor. 4:5.
11. 1 Cor. 4:21.
12. Ecclus. 32:1.
13. 1 Peter 5:3.
14. Mt 20:25–28.
15. Mt 24:48–51.
16. 1 Kings 2:29.
17. Ezek. 34:4.
18. *Mor.* 20. 5:14.
19. Cf. Luke 10:33 ff.
20. Cf. Heb. 9:4.
21. Ps. 22:4.

St. Bernard of Clairvaux

St. Bernard of Clairvaux (A.D. 1090–1153), whose charismatic and forceful personality can still be felt through his writings, earned renown both for his promotion of the Cistercian reform of Benedictine monasticism in the context of the ecclesiastical situation of his time, and for his theological treatises and commentaries. He wrote Five Books on Consideration ("books" being equivalent to modern chapters) to Pope Eugene III, who had been a monk at Clairvaux where St. Bernard was abbot. In this work, he explores the relationship of the active and contemplative life not simply theoretically, but in light of the practical realities of the Pope's day-to-day responsibilities. I have selected a passage in which St. Bernard emphasizes the need for the Pope to take time to pray and meditate upon the sources of the virtuous life in order to be able to accomplish the arduous task of governing his flock with justice.

IF WE WERE PERMITTED to do what we should, we would always, everywhere, and absolutely prefer that quality which is of value in every way and cherish it alone, or at least above all else. And this is piety, as irrefutable logic demonstrates. What is piety, you ask? To take time for consideration. Perhaps you may say that I differ in my definition from

From: Five Books on Consideration: Advice to a Pope, Book 1, trans. John D. Anderson and Elizabeth Kennan, Cistercian Fathers Series, no. 37: The Works of Bernard of Clairvaux, vol. 13 (Kalamazoo, Mich.: Cistercian Publications, 1976), 37–46.

the man who defined piety as worship of God. But that is not so. If you carefully consider, his meaning is expressed by my words, at least partially. For what is as integral to the worship of God as that which he himself urges in the Psalm: "Be still and know that I am God"? This certainly is the essence of consideration. What is as valuable as consideration which benevolently presumes to take part in an action by anticipating and planning what must be done? This is absolutely necessary. Affairs which have been thought out and planned in advance can be accomplished efficiently, but they can lead to great danger if done haphazardly. I have no doubt that you can recall frequent experiences of this kind of legal affairs, in important business matters, or in any deliberations of significance.

Now, of primary importance is the fact that consideration purifies its source, that is, the mind. Notice also that it controls the emotions, guides actions, corrects excesses, improves behavior, confers dignity and order on life, and even imparts knowledge of divine and human affairs. It puts an end to confusion, closes gaps, gathers up what has been scattered, roots out secrets, hunts down truth, scrutinizes what seems to be true, and explores lies and deceit. It decides what is to be done and reviews what has been done in order to eliminate from the mind anything deficient or in need of correction. Consideration anticipates adversity when all is going well and when adversity comes, it stands firm. In this it displays both prudence and fortitude.

Since you have just seen that prudence is the mother of fortitude, and that it is not fortitude but temerity to dare something that prudence has not conceived, observe the delightful and harmonious intermingling of the virtues and how one depends on the other. Prudence is the mean of desire and necessity, and like a judge it sets definite boundaries for both. For some it provides what is needed, for others it curtails what is excessive. In this way it forms a third virtue called temperance. Consideration judges intemperate both the man who obstinately denies himself necessities and the man who indulges in excess. Thus, temperance is not only the rejection of what is excessive, but also the acceptance of what is necessary. The Apostle seems not only to have promoted this idea, but to have originated it, for he teaches us not to provide for the flesh in its desires.[1] Indeed, when he says not to provide for the flesh, he moderates excess; when he adds, "in its desires," he admits necessities. Therefore, it seems to me not altogether absurd to define temperance as a virtue which neither excludes necessity nor exceeds it. As the Philosopher says, "Nothing in excess."

Now concerning justice, one of the four virtues, is it not a fact that consideration guides the mind into conformity with this virtue? For the mind must first reflect upon itself to deduce the norm of justice, which is not to do to another what one would not wish done to himself, nor deny another what one wishes for himself.[2] In these two rules the entire nature of justice is made clear. But justice is not a solitary virtue. Observe its exquisite connection and coherence with temperance and the likewise the relation of these two with the virtues discussed above, prudence and fortitude. Since the role of justice is said to consist in not doing to another what one does not want done to himself, the fulfillment of this virtue is expressed in the Lord's statement, "Whatever you wish men to do to you, do to them."[3] Neither of these is possible unless the will, which shapes them, is brought under control so that it neither desires anything excessive nor presumptuously avoids anything necessary. This is the role of temperance. Also, temperance sets a limit for justice in order to keep it just. The Wise Man confirms this when he says, "Do not be excessively just."[4] In this way he displays disapproval of justice which is not restrained and bridled by temperance. What is more, wisdom does not refuse the bridle of temperance. With the wisdom which God gave him, Paul says, "Do not let your wisdom go to extremes but let it be tempered by moderation."[5] But on the other hand, the Lord indicates that justice is necessary for temperance; in the Gospel he censures the temperance of those who fast so they may be seen fasting by men.[6] There was temperance in their food, but justice was not in their hearts, because they intended not to please God, but men.[7] And I repeat: how can you have either one of these without fortitude? It is fortitude's task, and no small task at that, to restrain one's likes and dislikes between the extremes of too little and too much so that the will can be content with this middle way which is bare, pure, solitary, consistent and self-contained, since it is equally isolated on every side; in short, the very essence of virtue.

Tell me if you can, to which of these three virtues you think we should especially attribute the mean, which is coterminous with them all in such a way that it seems proper to each? Or is the mean virtue itself? But then virtue would not be many-faceted, but all the virtues would be one. On the other hand, because no virtue is possible without it, is the mean somehow the essential core of the virtues in which all are united so as to appear as one? Certainly, they do not unite by sharing it, but each totally and perfectly possess it. For example, what is as essential to justice as the mean? Otherwise, if justice fails to attain the mean in all respects, it clearly does not give to each his due as it should. Similarly, what is as essential to temperance which is a virtue precisely because it allows nothing in excess? But I am sure you will admit that the mean is no less essential to fortitude, especially since it is this virtue which successfully rescues the mean unharmed from the onslaught of vices which try to strangle it, and establishes it as a solid foundation of goodness and seat of virtue. Therefore, to maintain the mean is justice, and it is temperance, and it is fortitude. But see whether they do not differ in this way: when an undertaking is in the will, it is within the sphere of justice; it is accomplished by fortitude; and it is maintained and utilized by temperance. It remains to show that prudence is not excluded from this union. Is it not this virtue which first discovers the mean and directs the mind toward it when that middle way has been long neglected and concealed by jealous vices and covered over by the darkness of time? This is why the mean is noticed by few people, because prudence is possessed by few. Thus, justice seeks; prudence finds. Fortitude lays claim; temperance possesses. I do not intend to discuss the virtues here, but I have said this much to encourage you to set aside for consideration which leads to the discovery of these virtues and others like them. To give no time during your life to such pious and beneficial leisure, is this not to lose your life?

But what can you do? If you suddenly devote yourself completely to this philosophy, although it is not customary for a pope to do so, you will indeed annoy many people. You will be like a person who abandons the footsteps of his ancestors, and this will be seen as an affront to them. You will be censured with the common saying, "Everyone wonders about the person who behaves differently." It will seem that you only want attention. You cannot suddenly correct every error at once or reduce excesses to moderation. There will be an opportunity at the proper time for you to pursue this little by little, according to the wisdom given you by God.[8] In the meantime, do what you can to utilize other people's evil for good. If we look for examples of good Roman Pontiffs and not just recent ones, we will discover some who found leisure in the midst of the most important affairs. When Rome was besieged and the barbarian sword threatened the necks of its citizens, did fear stop blessed Pope

Gregory from writing about wisdom in leisure? At that very time, as his preface reveals, he wrote his commentary on the very obscure final section of Ezekiel.[9] And he did this carefully and elegantly.

But let that be; a different custom has developed. The times and the habits of men are different now. Dangers are no longer imminent, they are present. Fraud, deceit, and violence run rampant in our land. False accusers are many; a defender is rare. Everywhere the powerful oppress the poor. We cannot abandon the downtrodden; we cannot refuse judgment to those who suffer injustice.[10] If cases are not tried and litigants heard, how can judgment be passed?

Let cases be tried, but in a suitable manner, for the way which is frequently followed now is completely detestable. It would hardly suit civil courts, let alone ecclesiastical. I am astonished that you, a man of piety, can bear to listen to lawyers dispute and argue in a way which tends more to subvert the truth than to reveal it. Reform this corrupt tradition; cut off their lying tongues and shut their deceitful mouths.[11] These men have taught their tongues to speak lies.[12] They are fluent against justice. They are schooled in falsehood. They are wise in order to do evil; they are eloquent to assail truth. These it is who instruct those by whom they should have been taught, who introduce not facts but their own fabrications, who heap up calumny of their own invention against innocent people, who destroy the simplicity of truth, who obstruct the ways of justice. Nothing reveals the truth so readily as a simple straightforward presentation. Therefore, let it be your custom to become involved in only those cases where it is absolutely necessary (and this will not be every case) and decide them carefully but briefly, and to avoid frustrating and contrived delays. The case of a widow requires your attention, likewise the case of a poor man and of one who has no means to pay. You can distribute many cases to others for judgment and many you can judge unworthy of a hearing. What need is there to hear those whose sins are manifest before the trial?

Some people are so impudent that, even when their case openly abounds with the itch of ambition, they are not embarrassed to demand a hearing. They flaunt themselves before the public conscience in a trial where they provide sufficient evidence to condemn themselves. There has been no one to restrain their hard-headedness and therefore they have multiplied and become even more set in their ways. I do not understand why, but the guilty are not shamed by the consciences of other guilty men; where all are filthy, the stench of one is hardly noticed. For example, are the greedy embarrassed before their own kind, the unclean before others like them, or the profligate before other profligates? The Church is filled with ambitious men; in our age she shudders at the calculated strivings of ambition no more than a den of thieves shudders at the spoils taken from travelers.

If you are Christ's disciple, let your zeal be enflamed and let your authority rise up against the widespread plague of this impudence. See what the Master did; hear what he says; "Let whoever serves me follow me."[13] He did not take time to listen, he took a whip to beat them. He neither spoke to them nor heeded their complaints. He did not sit and judge; he pursued and punished. Still, he was not silent about the reason: they had changed a house of prayer into a place of business.[14] Therefore, go and do likewise.[15] Let such businessmen embarrass you, if that is possible; if not, give them reason to fear. You too have a whip. Let the moneychangers be afraid, and not trust in their money, but lose confidence in it. Let them hide their money from you, knowing that you are more apt to throw it away than take it. If you do this with determination and perseverance you will win many who are greedy for gain and direct them to more honorable occupations. You will also save many by preventing them from even daring to attempt this sort of thing. In addition, this will greatly increase the leisure I am urging for you. You will save a great deal of time for consideration if you refuse to deal with some business and assign some to others, and decide faithfully and with due deliberation those cases which you feel merit a hearing. I think I will add some things about consideration, but after I begin the second book. Let the first one end here so that my treatise, which is hardly pleasant, will not additionally burden you by its length.

Questions for Bernard

1. How does "consideration" (that is, prayer and contemplation) purify and strengthen the mind?
2. Why is "consideration" necessary for possession of the virtues? Why should a busy priest, bishop, or Pope take time for prayer and contemplation?
3. Without such "consideration," why will the Pope be unable to administer justice?

Notes

1. Rom. 13:4.
2. Mt 7:12.
3. Mt 7:12.
4. Eccles. 7:17.
5. Rom. 12:13.
6. Mt 6:16.
7. Gal. 1:10.
8. 2 Pet. 3:15.
9. Homily on Ezekiel 2: preface; PL 76:934.
10. Ps 102:6; 145:7.
11. Ps 11:4.
12. Jer. 9:5.
13. Jn 12:26.
14. Mt 21:13.
15. Lk 10:37.

St. Thomas Aquinas

St. Thomas Aquinas (A.D. 1225–1274) is best known for his theological masterpiece, the *Summa Theologiae.* His biblical commentaries also deserve esteem. I offer here two passages from his "Commentary on the Gospel of St. John," one from the beginning of the Gospel (chapter 2, verses 14–17) and one from the end of the Gospel (chapter 21, verses 15–17). In these passages, St. Thomas's understanding of the priesthood is brilliantly illumined. The first passage treats corruption in the priesthood (especially among bishops), and discusses how such corruption should be handled. Note his powerful critique of Christian simony. The second passage addresses the authority of the Pope and bishops.

Chapter 2 of the Gospel of John: Lecture 2

(14) In the temple precincts he came upon merchants selling oxen, sheep, and doves, and moneychangers seated at tables. (15) And when he had made a kind of whip from cords, he drove everyone, including sheep and oxen, out of the temple, swept away the gold of the moneychangers, and

From: Commentary on the Gospel of John, trans. James A. Weisheipl, O.P., and Fabian R. Larcher, O.P., part 1 (Albany, N.Y.: Magi Books, 1980), 164–169, #380–392; trans. James A. Weisheipl, O.P., and Fabian R. Larcher, O.P., part 2 (Petersham, Mass.: St. Bede's Publications, 1999), 639–644, #2614–2627. Text appears courtesy of Magi Books and St. Bede's Publications.

knocked over their tables. (16) To those selling doves he said, "Get out of here! And stop making my Father's house into a marketplace." (17) His disciples then remembered that it is written: "Zeal for your house consumes me."

Then when he says, **In the temple precincts he came upon merchants selling oxen, sheep, and doves**, the Evangelist sets down what moved Christ to propose the sign of the resurrection. He does three things with this. First, he exposes the faulty behavior of the Jews. Secondly, he discloses Christ's remedy (v. 15). Thirdly, he gives the announcement of the prophecy (v. 22).

With respect to the first, we should note that the devil plots against the things of God and strives to destroy them. Now among the means by which he destroys holy things, the chief is avarice; hence it is said: "The shepherds have no understanding. All have turned aside to their own way; everyone after his own gain, from the first one to the last" (Is 56:11). And the devil has done this from the earliest times. For the priests of the Old Testament, who had been established to care for divine matters, gave free rein to avarice. God commanded, in the law, that animals should be sacrificed to the Lord on certain feasts. And in order to fulfill this command, those who lived nearby brought the animals with them. But those who came a long distance were unable to bring animals from their own homes. And so because offerings of this kind resulted in profit for the priests, and so animals to offer would not be lacking to those who came from a distance, the priests themselves saw to it that animals were sold in the temple. And so they had them shown for sale in the temple, i.e., in the atrium of the temple. And this is what he says: **In the temple precincts he came upon merchants selling oxen, sheep, and doves.**

Mention is first made of two land animals, which according to the law could be offered to the Lord: the ox and the sheep. The third land animal offered, the goat, is implied when he says "sheep"; similarly, the turtle-dove is included when he says "doves."

It sometimes happened that some came to the temple not only without animals, but also without money to buy them. And so the priests found another avenue for their avarice; they set up moneychangers who would lend money to those who came without it. And although they would not accept a usurious gain, because this was forbidden in the law, nevertheless in place of this they accepted certain "collibia," i.e., trifles and small gifts. So this also was turned to the profit of the priests. And this is what he says, **moneychangers seated at tables**, i.e., in the temple, ready to lend money.

This can be understood mystically in three ways. First of all, the merchants signify those who sell or buy the things of the Church: for the oxen, sheep, and doves signify the spiritual goods of the Church and the things connected with them. These goods have been consecrated and authenticated by the teachings of the apostles and doctors, signified by the oxen: "When there is an abundant harvest the strength of the ox is evident" (Prov. 14:4); and by the blood of the martyrs, who are signified by the sheep, so it is said for them: "We are regarded as sheep for the slaughter" (Rom. 8:36); and by the gifts of the Holy Spirit, signified by the doves, for as stated above, the Holy Spirit appeared in the form of a dove. Therefore, those who presume to sell the spiritual goods of the Church and the goods connected with them are selling the teachings of the apostles, the blood of the martyrs, and the gifts of the Holy Spirit.

Secondly, it happens that certain prelates or heads of churches sell these oxen, sheep, and doves, not overtly by simony, but covertly by negligence; that is, when they are so eager for and occupied with temporal gain that they neglect the spiritual welfare of their subjects. And this is the way they sell the oxen, sheep, and doves, i.e., the three classes of people subject to them. First of all, they sell the preachers and laborers, who are signified by the oxen: "Happy are you who sow beside all the streams, letting the ox and the donkey range free" (Is 32:20); because prelates ought to arrange the oxen, i.e., teachers and wise men, with the donkeys, i.e., the simple and uneducated. They also sell those in the active life, and those occupied with ministering, signified by the sheep: "My sheep hear my voice" (John 10:27); and as is said in 2 Samuel (24:17): "But these, who are the sheep, what have they done?" They also sell the contemplatives, signified by the doves: "Who will give me wings like a dove, and I will fly?" (Ps. 54:7).

Thirdly, by the temple of God we can understand the spiritual soul, as it says: "The temple of God is holy, and that is what you are" (1 Cor. 3:17). Thus a man sells oxen, sheep, and doves in the temple when he harbors bestial movements in his soul, for which he sells himself to the devil. For the oxen, which are used for cultivating the earth, signify earthly desires; sheep, which are stupid animals, signify man's obstinacy;

and the doves signify man's instability. It is God who drives these things out of men's hearts.

The Lord's remedy is at once set forth (v. 15). Here the Lord's remedy consisted in action and in words, in order to instruct those who have charge of the Church that they must correct their subjects in deed and in word. And he does two things with respect to this. First, he gives the remedy Christ applied by his action. Secondly, the remedy he applied by word (v. 16).

As to the first he does three things. First, he drives the men out. Secondly, the oxen and sheep. Thirdly, he sweeps away the money.

He drives the men out with a whip: and this is what he says, **when he had made a kind of whip from cords**. This is something that could be done only by divine power. For as Origen says, the divine power of Jesus was as able, when he willed, to quench the swelling anger of men as to still the storms of minds: "The Lord brings to nought the thoughts of men" (Ps. 32:10). He makes the whip from cords because, as Augustine says, it is from our own sins that he forms the matter with which he punishes us: for a series of sins, in which sins are added to sins, is called a cord: "He is bound fast by the cords of his own sins" (Prov. 5:22); "Woe to you who haul wickedness with cords" (Is 5:18). Then, just as he drove the merchants from the temple, so he swept away the gold of the moneychangers and knocked over their tables.

And mark well that if he expelled from the temple things that seemed somehow licit, in the sense that they were ordained to the worship of God, how much more if he comes upon unlawful things? The reason he cast them out was because in this matter the priests did not intend God's glory, but their own profit. Hence it is said: "It is for yourselves that you placed guardians of my service in my sanctuary" (Ez 44:8).

Further, our Lord showed zeal for the things of the law so that he might by this answer the chief priests and the priests who were later to bring a charge against him on this very point. Again, by casting things of this kind out of the temple he let it be understood that the time was coming in which the sacrifices of the law were due to cease, and the true worship of God transferred to the Gentiles: "The kingdom of God will be taken away from you" (Mt 21:43). Also, this shows us the condemnation of those who sell spiritual things: "May your money perish together with you" (Acts 8:20).

Then when he says, **To those selling doves he said**, he records the treatment which the Lord applied by word. Here it should be noted that those who engage in simony should, of course, first be expelled from the Church. But because as long as they are alive, they can change themselves by free will and by the help of God return to the state of grace, they should not be given up as hopeless. If, however, they are not converted, then they are not merely to be expelled, but handed over to those to whom it is said: "Bind him hand and foot, and cast him into outer darkness" (Mt 22:13). And so the Lord, attending to this, first warns them, and then gives the reason for his warning, saying, **stop making my Father's house into a marketplace**.

He warns those selling the doves by reproaching them, for they signify those who sell the gifts of the Holy Spirit, i.e., those who engage in simony.

He gives his reason for this when he says, **stop making my Father's house into a marketplace**. "Take away your evil from my sight" (Is 1:16). Note that Matthew (21:13) says: "Do not make my house a den of thieves," while here he says, **a marketplace**. Now the Lord does this because, as a good physician, he begins first with the gentler thing; later on, he would propose harsher things. Now the action recorded here was the first of the two; hence in the beginning he does not call them thieves but merchants. But because they did not stop such business out of obstinacy, the Lord, when driving them out the second time (as mentioned in Mark 11:15), rebukes them more severely, calling robbery what he had first called business.

He says, **my Father's house**, to exclude the error of Manicheus, who said that while the God of the New Testament was the Father of Christ, the God of the Old Testament was not. But if this were true, then since the temple was the house of the Old Testament, Christ would not have referred to the temple as **my Father's house**.

Why were the Jews not disturbed here when he called God his Father, for as is said below (John 5:18), this is why they persecuted him? I answer that God is the Father of certain men through adoption; for example, he is the Father of the just in this way. This was not a new idea for the Jews: "You will call me Father, and you will not cease to walk after me" (Jer. 3:19). However, by nature he is the Father of Christ alone: "The Lord said to me: 'You are my Son'" (Ps. 2:7), i.e., the true and natural Son. It is this that was unheard of among the Jews. And so the Jews persecuted him because he called himself the true Son of God: "The Jews tried all the harder to kill him, because he not only broke the Sabbath rest, but even called God his Father, making himself equal to God" (John 5:18). But when he called God his Father on this occasion, they said it was by adoption.

That the house of God shall not be made a marketplace is taken from Zechariah (14:21): "On that day there will no longer be any merchants in the house of the Lord of hosts"; and from the Psalm (70:16), where one version has the reading: "Because I was not part of the marketplace, I will enter into the strength of the Lord."

Then when he says, **His disciples then remembered**, he sets down a prophecy which was written in Psalm 69 (v. 9): "Zeal for your house consumes me." Here we should remark that zeal, properly speaking, signifies an intensity of love, whereby the one who loves intensely does not tolerate anything which is repugnant to his love. So it is that men who love their wives intensely and cannot endure their being in the company of other men, as this conflicts with their own love, are called "zelotypes." Thus, properly speaking, one is said to have zeal for God who cannot patiently endure anything contrary to the honor of God, whom he loves above all else: "I have been very zealous for the Lord God of hosts" (1 Kgs 19:10). Now we should love the house of the Lord, according to the Psalm (25:8): "O Lord, I have loved the beauty of your house." Indeed, we should love it so much that our zeal consumes us, so that if we notice anything amiss being done, we should try to eliminate it, no matter how dear to us are those who are doing it; nor should we fear any evils that we might have to endure as a result. So the Gloss says: "Good zeal is a fervor of spirit, by which, scorning the fear of death, one is on fire for the defense of the truth. He is consumed by it who takes steps to correct any perversity he sees; and if he cannot, he tolerates it with sadness."

Chapter 21 of the Gospel of John: Lecture 3

(15)When they had finished breakfast, Jesus said to Simon Peter, "Simon, son of John, do you love me more than these?" He said to him, "Yes, Lord; you know that I love you." He said to him, "Feed my lambs." (16) A second time he said to him, "Simon, Son of John, do you love me?" He said to him, "Yes, Lord; you know that I love you." He said to him, "Tend my sheep"

[Feed my lambs]. (17) He said to him the third time, "Simon, son of John, do you love me?" Peter was grieved because he said to him a third time, "Do you love me?" And he said to him, "Lord, you know everything; you know that I love you." Jesus said to him, "Feed my sheep."

The Evangelist just showed what the Lord did for the disciples in general; here he shows him dealing with his two especially loved disciples: first, what he did for Peter; and how he dealt with John (v. 20). He does two things with the first: first, he lays on Peter the pastoral office; secondly, he predicts that he will be martyred (v. 18).

He imposes the pastoral office on Peter only after an examination. Thus, those who are to be raised to this office are first examined, "Do not be hasty in the laying on of hands" (1 Tim. 5:22). Christ examined him three times, and so this part is divided into three parts. In the first part we see our Lord's question (v. 15); Peter's answer; and the imposition of the office (v. 15). Looking at the first, we can consider three things: the time of the examination; the tenor of the conversation; and on what Peter was examined.

The order of this event is given as **When they had finished the meal**. This signifies the spiritual meal by which the soul is refreshed with spiritual gifts, even when it is united to the body: "I will come in to him and eat with him" (Rev. 3:20). Therefore it is appropriate that one who is raised to this office be already refreshed with this joyous meal. Otherwise, how could he refresh the hungry ones that come to him: "I will feast the soul of the priests with abundance" (Jer. 31:14), with that abundance mentioned in Psalm 63:5: "My soul is feasted as with marrow and fat."

The tenor of the conversation is seen when he says, **Jesus said to Simon Peter**. Three things are given here which are necessary for prelate. First, obedience, when he says, **Simon**, which means obedient. A prelate needs to be obedient because one who does not know how to obey superiors does not know how to govern inferiors: "An obedient man will speak of victory" (Prov. 21:28). Secondly, a prelate needs knowledge, indicated by **Peter**, which means understanding. A prelate needs understanding for he is the appointed watchman, and one who is blind is a poor watchman: "His watchmen are blind" (Is 56:10); "Because you have rejected knowledge, I reject you from being a priest to me" (Hos. 4:6). Thirdly, a prelate needs grace, for he says **son of John**. Prelates need grace because if they do not have grace they do not have anything: "By the grace of God I am what I am" (1 Cor. 15:10); "And when they perceived the grace that was given to me, James and Cephas and John, who were reputed to be pillars, gave to me and Barnabas the right hand of fellowship" (Gal. 2:9).

The questions are about love; and Jesus asks, **Do you love me more than these?** This was a suitable question, for Peter had previously fallen, as we saw before, and it was not appropriate that he be preferred to the others until his sin was forgiven—which is only brought about by charity: "Love covers a multitude of sins" (1 Pet. 4:8); "Love covers all offences" (Prov. 10:12). So it was fitting that his charity be made known by this questioning, not indeed to him who looks into the depths of our hearts, but to others. So Christ said, but not as one who did now already know, **Do you love me more than these?** Now we read that "perfect love casts out fear" (1 Jn 4:18). Thus it was that when our Lord was about to die, Peter was afraid and denied him; but the risen Lord restored love and banished his fear. So Peter, who before had denied Christ because he was afraid to die, now, after our Lord has arisen, feared nothing. Why should he be afraid, since he now realized that death had died?

This questioning was also appropriate for the office, since many who assume a pastoral office use it as self-lovers: "In the last days there will come times of stress. For men will be lovers of self" (1 Tim. 3:1). One who does not love the Lord is not a fit prelate. A fit prelate is one who does not seek his own advantage, but that of Christ's; and he does this through love: "The love of Christ controls us" (2 Cor. 5:14). Love also becomes this office because it benefits others: for it is due to the abundance of love that those who love Jesus will at times give up the quiet of their own contemplation to help their neighbor. Although the Apostle said, "I am sure that neither death nor life . . . will be able to separate us from the love of God" (Rom. 8:39), he added, "For I could wish that I myself were accursed and cut off from Christ for the sake of my brethren" (Rom. 9:3). Thus a prelate should be questioned about his love.

He adds, **more than these**, for even as the Philosopher says in his *Politics*, it is the natural order of things that the one who cares for and governs others should be better. Thus he says that just as the soul is to the body that it rules, and reason is to our lower powers, so man is related to the irrational animals. And there ought to be a similar relation between prelates and their subjects. Thus, according to Gregory, the life of a pastor should be such that he is related to his subjects as a shepherd to his sheep. So Christ says, **more than these**, because the more Peter loves the better he is: "Do you see him whom the Lord has chosen? There is none like him among all the people" (1 Sam. 10:24).

But in selecting someone [to rule] is it always necessary to choose the one who is unconditionally better, even if the laws say that it is enough to choose one who is merely good? To answer this two distinctions must be made. Some things are sufficient according to human judgment which are still not sufficient for his election to stand. For it is obvious that it would be difficult to have elections if they could be nullified because someone was found who was better than the one actually chosen. So, according to our human judgment, it is sufficient if an election is honest and a suitable person is chosen.

But, so far as concerns the divine judgment, and our own conscience, it is necessary to choose that person who is better. Now a person can be unconditionally better; and this is the way a holier person is said to be better, for holiness makes one good. Yet such a person might not be better for the Church. For this purpose, that person would be better educated, more competent, more discerning, and chosen more unanimously. But if other things are equal, such as the benefit and welfare of the Church, one would sin if he were to choose a person who was less unconditionally good than another. There has to be a reason for such a choice. This is either the honor of God and the benefit of the Church, or some private motive. If the motive is the honor of God and the benefit to the Church, these goods will be regarded as linked to the one chosen, and will make him the better person, in these respects. If there is some private motive for the choice, such as some carnal love, the expectation of ecclesiastical advancement, or temporal advantage, the election is a fraud and there has been partiality.

Now we see Peter's answer, **Yes, Lord; you know that I love you**. This is a clear sign that he had retracted his previous denial. And it shows that if the predestined fall, they are always better after they are corrected. Before his denial, Peter thought that he was better than the other apostles, saying, "Though they all fall away because of you, I will never fall away" (Mt 26:33). And when Jesus said to him, "You will deny me three times," Peter went against this and even boasted that "Even if I must die with you, I will not deny you" (Mt 26:35). But now, Peter, having been conquered by his own weakness, does not presume to state his love unless it is attested to and confirmed by the Lord. He humbles himself before Christ, saying, **You know that I love you**: "My witness is in heaven, and he that vouches for me is on high" (Job 16:19). He also humbles himself in respect to the apostles, for he does not say that he loves Jesus more than they do, but simply, I love you. This teaches us not to rank ourselves before others, but others before ourselves: "In humility count others better than yourselves" (Phil. 2:3).

We can also notice, as Augustine points out, that when our Lord asks, **Do you love** (*diligis*) me, Peter does not answer with the same word, but says I love (*amo*) you, as if they were the same. And they are the same in reality, but there is some difference in meaning: Love (*amor*) is a movement of our appetitive power, and if this is regulated by our reason it is the will's act of love, which is called "direction" (*dilectio*)—because it presupposes an act of election, choice (*electio*). This is why the brute animals are not said to love (*diligere*). For if the appetitive movement is not regulated by reason, it is called *amor*.

After this examination, Christ assigns Peter his office, saying **Feed my lambs**, that is my faithful, which I, the Lamb, call lambs: "Behold, the Lamb of God" (John 1:29). Thus, one should not be called a Christian who says he is not under the care of that shepherd, that is, Peter: "They shall all have one shepherd" (Ez 37:24); "They shall appoint for themselves one head" (Hos. 1:11). It was appropriate that this office be assigned to Peter, the others being passed over, because, according to Chrysostom, he was the extraordinary apostle, the voice of the disciples, and the head of the group.

Now we have the second examination. In order to avoid a lot of repetition, note that Christ says three times, **Feed my lambs**, because Peter ought to feed them three ways. First, they are to be fed by being taught: "And I will give you shepherds after my own heart, who will feed you with knowledge and understanding" (Jer. 3:15). Secondly, they are to be fed by example: "Set the believers an example in speech and conduct, in love, in faith, in purity" (1 Tim. 4:12); "Upon the mountain heights of Israel," that is, the excellence of great men, "shall be their pasture" (Ez 34:14). Thirdly, they are to be fed by being offered temporal help: "Woe, shepherds of Israel who have been feeding yourselves! Should not shepherds feed the sheep?" (Ez 34:2).

The third time Christ says to him, **Feed my sheep**. This is because there are three types of people in the Church: beginners, those who have made some progress, and the perfect. The first two types are the lambs, since they are still imperfect. The others, since they are perfect, are called sheep: "The mountains," that is, the perfect, "skipped like rams," and "the hills," the others, "like lambs" (Ps. 114:4). And so all prelates ought to guard their charges as Christ's sheep and not their own. But alas! As Augustine says in his *Easter Sermon*: "We witness the appearance of certain unfaithful servants who have abandoned Christ's flock and by their thefts have made gold their flock. You hear them say, 'These are my sheep. What do you want with my sheep? I will not let you come to my sheep.' But if we say 'my sheep,' and others talk about their sheep, then Christ has lost his own sheep."

Note also that just as Peter was assigned his office three times, so he was examined three times. This was because he had denied Christ three times. As Augustine says: "A threefold profession was required so that Peter's tongue might show as much love as it had shown of fear, and that life gained would wrest more words that the threat of death." Another reason for this was because Peter was obligated to love Christ for three things. First, because his sin was forgiven, for the one who is forgiven more loves the more (cf. Lk 7:43). Secondly, because he was promised a great honor: "On this rock I will build my Church" (Mt 16:18). Thirdly, because of the office entrusted to him, as right here, when Christ entrusts the care of the Church to him, **Feed**. "You shall love the Lord your God with all your heart," so that you will direct your entire intention to God, "and with all your soul," so that your entire will might rest in God through love, "and with all your might," so that the performance of all your actions will serve God.

Peter became sad because he was asked three times. As was seen, he was rebuked by our Lord before the passion when he so quickly asserted that he loved him. Now, seeing that he is questioned so many times about his love, he is afraid he will be rebuked again and becomes sad. Thus he says, **Lord, you know everything; you know that I love you**. He is saying in effect: I do love you; at least I think I do. But you know all things, and perhaps you know of something else that will happen. And so the final commitment of the Church is given to the humbled Peter. According to one of the Greek doctors, this is also the reason why catechumens are questioned three times during their baptism.

Questions for Aquinas

1. How does Aquinas, interpreting Christ's condemnation of the merchants and moneychangers in the Temple, direct this condemnation against those bishops of his own day who engaged in simony and were preoccupied with gaining worldly wealth?
2. How should zeal motivate believers?
3. What qualities, according to Aquinas, are required for pastoral office? How should pastors "feed" their flock?

St. Catherine of Siena

St. Catherine of Siena (A.D. 1347–1380) composed *The Dialogue* in 1378, in the middle of a period of chaos in the Church's history. Between 1309 and 1377, the popes were in Avignon rather than in Rome. St. Catherine of Siena helped to persuade Pope Gregory XI to return to Rome in 1377. In 1378, however, Gregory XI died and the Great Schism, during which there were various rival claimants to the papacy, began (it did not end until 1417). *The Dialogue*, a theological masterpiece, earned St. Catherine her place as a Doctor or teacher of the Church. This excerpt comes from the section devoted to "The Mystic Body of Holy Church." In this section, God speaks to St. Catherine about the dignity of the priesthood and about the effects of corruption in the priesthood. Note the passionate intensity of the call to holiness.

O DEAREST DAUGHTER, I HAVE told you all this so that you may better know how I have dignified my ministers, and thus grieve the more over their wickedness. If they themselves had considered their dignity, they would not have fallen into the darkness of deadly sin nor muddied the face of their souls. Not only have they sinned against me and against their own dignity, but even had they given their bodies to be burned they would not have been able to repay me for the tremendous grace and

From: Excerpts from *The Dialogue*, trans. by Suzanne Noffke, O.P., in Classics of Western Spirituality Series copyright © 1980, used with permission of Paulist Press. *www.paulistpress.com*.

blessing they have received, for it is impossible to have a greater dignity than theirs in this life.

They are my anointed ones and I call them my "christs," because I have appointed them to be my ministers to you and have sent them like fragrant flowers into the mystic body of holy Church. No angel has this dignity, but I have given it to those men whom I have chosen to be my ministers. I have sent them like angels, and they ought to be earthly angels in this life.

I demand purity and charity of every soul, a charity that loves me and others, and helps others in whatever way it can, serving them in prayer and loving them tenderly. But much more do I demand purity in my ministers, and that they love me and their neighbors, administering the body and blood of my only-begotten Son with burning love and hunger for the salvation of souls, for the glory and praise of my name.

Just as these ministers want the chalice in which they offer this sacrifice to be clean, so I demand that they themselves be clean in heart and soul and mind. And I want them to keep their bodies, as instruments of the soul, in perfect purity. I do not want them feeding and wallowing in the mire of impurity, nor bloated with pride in their hankering after high office, nor cruel to themselves and their neighbors—for they cannot abuse themselves without abusing their neighbors. If they abuse themselves by sinning, they are abusing the souls of their neighbors. For they are not giving them an example of good living, nor are they concerned about rescuing souls from the devil's hands, nor about administering to them the body and blood of my only-begotten Son, and myself the true Light in the other sacraments of holy Church. So, by abusing themselves they are abusing others.

I want them to be generous, not avariciously selling the grace of my Holy Spirit to feed their own greed.[1] They ought not do so; I will not have them do so. Rather, as they have received charity freely and generously from my goodness, so ought they to give to everyone who humbly asks, lovingly, freely, and with a generous heart, moved by love for my honor and the salvation of souls.[2] Nor ought they to take anything in payment for what they themselves have not bought but have received gratuitously so that they might administer it to you. But alms they may and should accept. So also should those act who are the receivers, for their part giving alms when they are able. For my ministers ought to be provided by you with material help in their needs, and you ought to be provided for and nourished by them with grace and spiritual gifts, that is, with the holy sacraments I have established in holy Church for them to administer to you for your salvation.[3]

And I want you to know that they give you incomparably more than you give them, for there is no comparison between the finite and passing things with which you help them, and myself, God, who am infinite and have appointed them in my providence and divine charity to minister to you. With all of your material possessions you could never repay the incomparable spiritual gifts you receive—not only this mystery, but everything whatever that is administered to you by anyone as a spiritual favor, whether through prayer or any other means.

Now I tell you that whatever my ministers receive from you they are obliged to distribute in three ways by dividing it into three parts: one for their own livelihood, one for the poor, and the rest for what is needed for the Church. If they use it in any other way they would offend me.

This is how my gentle glorious ministers conduct themselves. I told you that I wanted you to see the excellence that is theirs beyond the dignity I have given them by making them my christs. When they exercise the dignity virtuously they are clothed in this gentle glorious Sun that I have entrusted to their ministry.

Consider those who have gone before them: the gentle Gregory, Sylvester,[4] and the other successors of the chief pontiff Peter, to whom my Truth gave the keys of the heavenly kingdom when he said, "Peter, I am giving you the keys of the heavenly kingdom; whatever you loose on earth shall be loosed in heaven, and whatever you bind on earth shall be bound in heaven."[5]

Listen well, dearest daughter. By showing you the magnificence of their virtues I shall show you more fully the dignity to which I have appointed these ministers of mine. This is the key[6] to the blood of my only-begotten Son, that key which unlocked eternal life, closed for so long a time because of Adam's sin. But after I gave you my Truth, the Word, my only-begotten Son, he suffered and died, and by his death he destroyed your death[7] by letting his blood be a cleansing bath for you. Thus his blood and his death, by the power of my divine nature joined with his human nature, unlocked eternal life.

And to whom did he leave the keys to this blood? To the glorious apostle Peter and to all the others who have come or will come from now until the final judgment day with the very same authority that Peter had.

Nor is this authority lessened by any sinfulness on their part; nor can that sinfulness deprive the blood or any other sacrament of its perfection. I have already told you that no uncleanness can defile this Sun, nor is its light lost because of any darkness of deadly sin that may be in the minister or in those who receive it. Their sin cannot injure the sacraments of holy Church or lessen their power. But grace is lessened and sin increased in those who administer or receive them unworthily.

Christ on earth,[8] then, has the keys to the blood. If you remember, I showed you this in an image when I wanted to teach you the respect laypeople ought to have for these ministers of mine, regardless of how good or evil they may be, and how displeased I am with disrespect. You know that I set before you the mystic body of the holy Church under the image of a wine cellar. In this wine cellar was the blood of my only-begotten Son, and from this blood all the sacraments derive their life-giving power.

Christ on earth stood at the door of this wine cellar. He had been commissioned to administer the blood, and it was his duty to delegate ministers to help him in the service of the entire universal body of Christianity. Only those accepted and anointed by him were to thus minister. He was the head of the whole clerical order, and he appointed each one to his proper office to administer this glorious blood.

Because he has sent them out as his helpers, it is his task to correct them for their faults, and it is my will that he do so. For by the dignity and authority I have bestowed on them I have freed them from slavery, that is, from submission to the authority of temporal rulers. Civil law has no power whatever to punish them; this right belongs solely to the one who has been appointed to rule and to serve according to divine law. There are my anointed ones, and therefore it has been said through Scripture: "Dare not to touch my christs."[9] Therefore, a person can do no worse violence than to assume the right to punish my ministers.[10]

And if you should ask me why I said that this sin of those who persecute holy Church is graver than any other sin, and why it is my will that the sins of the clergy should not lessen your reverence for them, this is how I would answer you: because the reverence you pay to them is not actually paid to them but to me, in virtue of the blood I have entrusted to their ministry. If this were not so, you should pay them as much reverence as to anyone else, and no more. It is this ministry of theirs that dictates that you should reverence them and come to them, not for what they are in themselves but for the power I have entrusted to them, if you would receive the holy sacraments of the Church. For if you refuse these when it is in your power to have them, you would live and die condemned.

So the reverence belongs not to the ministers, but to me and to this glorious blood made one thing with me because of the union of divinity with humanity. And just as the reverence is done to me, so also is the irreverence, for I have already told you that you must not reverence them for themselves, but for the authority I have entrusted to them. Therefore you must not sin against them, because if you do, you are really sinning not against them but against me. This I have forbidden, and I have said that it is my will that no one should touch them.

For this reason no one has excuse to say, "I am doing no harm, nor am I rebelling against holy Church. I am simply acting against the sins of evil pastors." Such persons are deluded, blinded as they are by their own selfishness. They see well enough, but they pretend not to see so as to blunt the prickling of conscience. If they would look, they could see that they are persecuting not these ministers, but the blood. It is me they assault, just as it was me they reverenced. To me redounds every assault they make on my ministers: derision, slander, disgrace, abuse. Whatever is done to them I count as done to me. For I have said and I say it again: No one is to touch my christs. It is my right to punish them, and no one else's.

But the wicked show how little they reverence the blood, how little they value the treasure I have given them for their souls' life and salvation. You could receive no greater gift than that I should give you myself, wholly God and wholly human, as your food.

But by not paying me reverence in the persons of my ministers, they have lost respect for the latter and persecuted them because of the many sins and faults they saw in them. If in truth the reverence they had for them had been for my sake, they would not have cut it off on account of any sin in them. For no sin can lessen the power of this sacrament, and therefore their reverence should not lessen either. When it does, it is against me they sin.

There are many reasons that make this sin more serious than any other, but I will tell you of three principal ones.

The first is that what they do to my ministers they do to me.[11]

The second is that they are violating my command, for I forbade them to touch [my christs]. They scorn the power of the blood they received in holy baptism, for they disobediently do what I have forbidden. They are rebels against the blood because they have become irreverent persecutors, like rotten members cut off from the mystic body of holy Church. And if they persist in this irreverent rebellion and die in it, they will end in eternal damnation. Still, if even at the end they humble themselves and admit their sin and want to be reconciled with their head—even though they cannot do it actually—they will receive mercy. But let no one count on having the time for this, since no one can be certain of it.

The third reason this sin is more serious than any other is that it is committed deliberately and with selfish malice. They know they cannot do it in good conscience, but they do it nonetheless and sin. And it is a sin committed in perverse pride without any bodily pleasure: Indeed, both body and soul are eaten up by it. Their souls are eaten up because they are deprived of grace and chewed up by the worm of conscience. Their material possessions are consumed in the service of the devil. And their bodies die of it like animals.

So this sin is committed directly against me. It is unmitigated by any profit to the sinner or any pleasure except the sooty spite of pride—a pride born of selfish sensuality and of that perverse slavish fear that led Pilate to kill Christ, my only-begotten Son, rather than risk losing his power. So do these behave.[12]

All other sins are committed either through stupidity or ignorance or through the sort of malice that, though conscious of the evil being done, sins for the sake of disordered pleasure or profit. Such sinners bring harm to their own soul and offend me and their neighbors—me because they are not praising and glorifying my name, their neighbors because they are not giving them the joy of their charity. But they are not actually persecuting me, because while they are sinning against me, it is themselves they are harming, and their sin displeases me because of the harm it does to them.

But this other is a sin committed directly against me. Other sins have some pretext; they are committed with some excuse, with some middle ground—for I told you that every sin as well as every virtue is realized for God and your neighbors, and virtue is practiced out of the warmth of charity. If you sin against your neighbors you sin against me through them.

But among all my creatures I have chosen these ministers of mine. They are my anointed ones, stewards of the body and blood of my only-begotten Son—your human flesh joined with my divinity. When they consecrate, they stand in the place of Christ my son. So you see, this sin is directed against this Word, and because it is done to him it is done to me, because we are one and the same. These wretches persecute the blood and so deprive themselves of the treasure and fruit of the blood. Thus I consider this sin, committed not against my ministers but against me, the more serious because the persecution as well as the honor is not (nor do I so consider it) owed to them but to me, that is, to this glorious blood of my Son, for we are one and the same. Therefore I tell you, if all the other sins these people have committed were put on one side and this one sin on the other, the one would weigh more in my sight than all the others. I have shown you this so that you would have more reason to grieve that I am offended and these wretched souls damned, so that the bitter sorrow of you and my other servants by my kind mercy might dissolve the great darkness that has come over these rotten members who are cut off from the mystic body of holy Church.

But I find hardly anyone who will grieve over the persecution that is waged against this glorious precious blood, while there are many who persecute me constantly with the arrows of disordered love and slavish fear and self-conceit. Blind as they are, they count as honor what is shameful, and as shame what is honorable, that is, to humble themselves before their head.

Through these sins they have risen up and continue to rise up to persecute the blood. I spoke the truth when I told you that they are persecuting me. So far as their intention is concerned, they persecute me in whatever way they can. Not that I in myself can be harmed or persecuted by them, for I am like the rock that is not hurt by what is thrown at it, but glances it back at the one who threw it.[13] Just so, the impact of the filthy sins they hurl can do me no harm, but their arrows glance back at them poisoned with guilt. This guilt deprives them of grace in this life because they lose the fruit of the blood, and in the end, unless they change their ways through heartfelt contrition and holy confession, they will come to eternal damnation, cut off from me and bound over to the devil. They have, in fact, made a compact, they and the devil, for as soon as they have lost grace they are bound in sin with the chain of hatred for virtue and love of vice. And this chain they have put into the devil's hands with their free choice. This is what he binds them with, for in no other way could they be bound.

This chain binds the persecutors of the blood one with the other, and as members bound up with the devil they have taken on the function of the devils. The devils make every effort to lead my creatures astray, to lure them away from grace and drag them down into the guilt of deadly sin, so that others may share the evil that is in themselves. This is what such people do, neither more nor less. As the devil's members they go about undermining the children of the bride of Christ, my only-begotten Son, undoing them from the bond of charity and binding them up in the wretched chain where they will be deprived of the fruit of the blood along with themselves. The links of this chain are pride and self-importance, along with the slavish fear that makes them lose grace rather than risk losing their temporal powers. So they fall into greater confusion than ever, since they have forfeited the honor of the blood. Their chain is welded with the seal of darkness, they have fallen and are making others fall. This is why they do not change their ways. They do not know themselves, but blind as they are they take pride in their own spiritual and bodily ruin.

O dearest daughter, grieve without measure at the sight of such wretched blindness in those who, like you, have been washed in the blood, have nursed and been nourished with this blood at the breast of holy Church! Now like rebels they have pulled away from that breast out of fear and under the pretext of correcting the faults of my ministers—something I have forbidden them to do, for I do not want [my anointed ones] touched by them. What terror should come over you and my other servants when you hear any mention of that wretched chain of theirs! Your tongue could never describe how hateful it is to me! And worse still, they want to take cover under the cloak of my ministers' sins so as to cover up their own sins. They forgot that no cloak can hide anything from my sight. They might well be able to hide from creatures, but not from me, for nothing present nor anything at all can be hidden from me. I loved you and knew you before you came into being.

And this is one reason the wicked of this world do not change their ways: They do not believe in truth, by the light of living faith, that I see them. For if they believed in truth that I see them and their sins, and that every sin is punished and every good rewarded, they would not commit such evil but would turn away from what they have done and humbly ask for my mercy. And I, through my Son's blood, would be merciful to them. But they are obstinate, and so they are rejected by my goodness and because of their sins fall into the ultimate disaster of losing the light and, blind as they are, becoming persecutors of the blood. But no fault on the part of the ministers of the blood can justify such persecution.

I have told you, dearest daughter, something of the reverence that ought to be given my anointed ones no matter how sinful they may be. For reverence neither is nor should be given them for what they are in themselves, but only the authority I have entrusted to them. The sacramental mystery cannot be lessened or divided by their sinfulness. Therefore your reverence for them should never fail—not for their own sake, but because of the treasure of the blood.

Looking to the contrary, I have shown you ever so little how grave and displeasing to me and how harmful to themselves is the irreverence of those who persecute the blood. And I have shown you the compact they have made against me by binding themselves together in the service of the devil, so that you may grieve the more.

I have told you specifically about this sin because of the persecution of holy Church. And I tell you the same of Christianity in general: Anyone who lives in deadly sin is scorning the blood and letting go of the life of grace. But much more displeasing to me and serious for themselves is the sin of those of whom I have spoken specifically.

Now I would refresh your soul by softening your grief over the darksomeness of those wretched ones with the holy lives of my ministers. I have told you that they have taken on the qualities of the Sun, so that the fragrance of their virtues mitigates the stench, and their lightsomeness the dark. By this very light I would have you know more deeply the sinful darksomeness of those other ministers of mine. So open your mind's eye and contemplate me, the Sun of justice, and you shall see these glorious ministers who by their stewardship of the Sun have taken on the qualities of the Sun.

I have told you about Peter, the prince of the apostles, who received the keys of the heavenly kingdom. Just so, I am telling you about others who, in this garden of holy Church, have been stewards of the light, that is, the body and blood of my only-begotten Son. He is the one undivided Sun, and all the Church's sacraments derive their value and life-giving power from his blood. All these of whom I am now telling you were appointed by rank according to their state to be stewards of the Holy Spirit's grace. How have they administered it? By the gracious brightness they have drawn from this true light.

Does this brightness exist by itself? No, for neither can the brightness of grace exist by itself nor can its light be divided: One must either have it whole and entire or not have it at all. Anyone living in deadly sin is by that very fact deprived of the light of grace. And anyone who has grace is spiritually enlightened by knowing me, for I am the giver of grace and of the virtue by which grace is preserved. It is in this light that the soul recognizes the wretchedness of sin and its source, sensual selfishness, and therefore hates it. By hating sin and its source she receives the warmth of divine charity into her will, for the will follows understanding. And she receives the color of this glorious light by following the teaching of my gentle Truth, whence her memory is filled in pondering the blessing of his blood.

So you see, it is impossible to receive this light without also receiving its warmth and color, for all three are fused into one and the same thing. Thus it is that the soul cannot have one of her powers disposed to receive me, the true Sun, unless all three of her powers are disposed together in my name. For as soon as the eye of understanding rises above physical sight by the light of faith and contemplates me, the will follows by loving what the eye of understanding has come to see and know, and the memory is filled with what the will loves. And as soon as these three powers are ready, the soul shares in me, the Sun, by being enlightened by my power and the wisdom of my only-begotten Son and the mercy of the Holy Spirit's fire.

So you see, the soul's powers have taken on the qualities of the sun. In other words, once these powers have been filled and clothed with me, the true Sun, they behave as the sun does. The sun warms and enlightens, and with its heat makes the earth bring forth fruit. So also these gentle ministers of mine, whom I chose and anointed and sent into the mystic body of holy Church to be stewards of me the Sun, that is, of the body and blood of my only-begotten Son along with the other sacraments that draw life from this blood. They administer it both actually and spiritually by giving off within the mystic body of holy Church the brightness of supernatural learning, the color of a holy and honorable life in following the teaching of my Truth, and the warmth of blazing charity. Thus with their warmth they cause barren souls to bring forth fruit, and enlighten them with the brightness of learning. By their holy and well-ordered lives they drive out the darksomeness of deadly sin and unfaithfulness, and set in order the lives of those who had been living disordered lives in the darkness of sin and the cold that came of their lack of charity. So you see how these ministers of mine are suns because they have taken on the qualities of me the true Sun. By love they have been made to be one thing with me and I with them.

They have all, according to the positions I have chosen them for, given light to holy Church: Peter with his preaching and teaching and in the end with his blood; Gregory with his learning and [his knowledge of] Sacred Scripture and the mirror of his living; Sylvester by his struggles against unbelievers and above all in the disputations and argumentations for the holy faith that he made in deeds as well as in words with the power he received from me. And if you turn to Augustine, to the glorious Thomas, to Jerome and the others, you will see what great light they have shed on this bride, as lamps set on a lamp-stand, dispelling errors with their true and perfect humility.

Hungry as they were for my honor and the salvation of souls, they fed on these at the table of the most holy cross. The martyrs did it with their blood. Their blood was fragrant to me, and with the fragrance of their blood and their virtues and with the light of learning they bore fruit in this bride. They spread the faith: Those who had been in darkness came to their light and they enkindled the light of faith in them. The prelates, who were entrusted with the authority of Christ on earth, offered me the just sacrifice of their holy and honorable lives. The pearl of justice shone in them and in their subjects, but first of all in them, with true humility and blazing charity, with enlightened discernment. Justly they offered me my due of glory and praise and offered themselves their contempt for their selfish sensuality by shunning vice and embracing virtue with charity for me and for their neighbors. With humility they trampled pride underfoot and like angels approached the table of the altar. They celebrated [the Mass] with bodily purity and spiritual sincerity, set ablaze as they were in charity's furnace. Because they had first done justice to themselves, they were just to their subjects as well. They wanted them to live virtuously, and so corrected them without any slavish fear, for their concern was not for themselves but only for my honor and the salvation of souls. They conducted themselves as good shepherds and followers of the good shepherd, my Truth, whom I sent to govern you, my little sheep, and to lay down his life for you.[14]

These ministers of mine followed in his footsteps. Therefore they did not let my members grow rotten for want of correction. But they corrected lovingly, with the ointment of kindness along with the harshness of the fire that cauterizes the wound of sin through reproof and penance, now more, now less, according to the gravity of the sin. Nor did it concern them that such correcting and speaking the truth might bring them death.

They were true gardeners, and with care and holy fear they rooted out the brambles of deadly sin and put in their place the fragrant plants of virtue. Thus their subjects lived in truly holy fear and they grew up as fragrant flowers in the mystic body of holy Church because my ministers fearlessly gave them the correction they needed. Because there was in them no thorn of sin, they kept to the way of holy justice and administered reproof without any slavish fear. This was and is the shining pearl that sheds peace and light on people's spirits and establishes them in holy fear with hearts united. I want you, therefore, to know that nothing causes as much darkness and division in the world among both laypeople and religious, clergy and shepherds of holy Church, as does the lack of the light of justice and the invasion of the darkness of injustice.

No rank, whether of civil or divine law, can be held in grace without holy justice.[15] For those who are not corrected and those who do not correct are like members beginning to rot, and if the doctor were only to apply ointment without cauterizing the wound, the whole body would become fetid and corrupt.

So it is with prelates or with anyone else in authority. If they see the members who are their subjects rotting because of the filth of deadly sin and apply only the ointment of soft words without reproof, they will never get well. Rather, they will infect the other members with whom they form one body under their one shepherd. But if those in authority are truly good doctors to those souls, as were those glorious shepherds, they will not use ointment without the fire of reproof. And if the members are still obstinate in their evildoing, they will cut them off from the congregation so that they will not infect the whole body with the filth of deadly sin.

But [those who are in authority] today do not do this. In fact, they pretend not to see. And do you know why? Because the root of selfish love is alive in them, and this is the source of their perverse slavish fear. They do not correct people for fear of losing their rank and position and their material possessions. They act as if they were blind, so they do not know how to maintain their positions. For if they saw how it is by holy justice that their positions are to be maintained, they would maintain them. But because they are bereft of light they do not know this. They believe they can succeed through injustice, by not reproving the sins of their subjects. But they are deceived by their own sensual passion, by their hankering for civil or ecclesiastical rank.

Another reason they will not correct others is that they themselves are living in the same or greater sins. They sense that the same guilt envelopes them, so they cast aside fervor and confidence and, chained by slavish fear, pretend they do not see. Even what they do see they do not correct, but let themselves be won over by flattery and bribes, using these very things as excuses for not punishing the offenders. In them is fulfilled what my Truth said in the holy Gospel: "They are blind and leaders of the blind. And if one blind person leads another, they both fall into the ditch."[16]

Those who have been or would be my gentle ministers did not and would not act this way. I told you that these have taken on the qualities of the sun. Indeed, they are suns, for there is in them no darkness of sin or ignorance, because they follow the teaching of my Truth. Nor are they lukewarm, because they are set ablaze in the furnace of my charity. They have no use for the world's honors and ranks and pleasures. Therefore, they are not afraid to correct. Those who do not hanker after power or ecclesiastical rank have no fear of losing it. They reprove [sin] courageously, for those whose conscience does not accuse them of sin have nothing to fear.

Questions for Catherine

1. What is the great dignity that God has given his ministerial priests? Explain how the sacraments are central to Catherine's understanding of the priesthood.
2. Why does Catherine warn against the laity condemning and disrespecting even sinful priests? What does Catherine fear will happen if priests, ordained by Christ's power, no longer have respect in the Church?
3. Having insisted upon the dignity of even sinful priests, Catherine also warns strongly against the sinfulness of priests. What happens when sinful priests fail to discipline their flocks?

Notes

1. Cf. Acts 8:18–20.

2. Cf. Mt 10:8.

3. Cf. 1 Cor. 9:11.

4. St. Gregory the Great, who was Pope from 590 to 604, and St. Sylvester I, 314 to 335.

5. Mt 16:19.

6. There is a double image here. Christ's blood is the key to eternal life. This key, his blood, is in turn locked within the "wine cellar" of the Church's "mystic body" (the sacramental heart of the Church), to which the pope holds the key. He unlocks the wine cellar and appoints ministers to carry the blood (the sacraments) to the people.

7. Cf. "Preface for Easter": "by dying he destroyed our death" (now one of the Acclamations after the Consecration of the Mass: "Dying you destroyed our death; rising you restored our life; Lord Jesus, come in glory!").

8. "Christ on earth" is Catherine's favorite name for the Pope as Christ's vicar.

9. Ps. 105:15.

10. This passage reflects the prevailing Church–state relationship of the Middle Ages, a relationship that was being severely challenged at the time the *Dialogue* was being written. This challenge was, in fact, at the root of the struggles between the papacy and the Italian city-states that Catherine tried so desperately to mediate.

11. Cf. Lk 10:16.

12. Cf. Jn 19:12.

13. Cf. Prov. 26:27. "A stone will come back on the person who starts it rolling."

14. Cf. Jn 10:11.

15. Cf. Prov. 16:12.

16. Mt 15:14; Lk 6:39.

St. Thomas More

After having served as a member of Parliament, a lawyer, and personal secretary to the king, St. Thomas More (A.D. 1478–1535) became Chancellor of England in 1529. A prolific author on political and ecclesial subjects, and a noted humanist (the Dutch humanist and classical scholar Erasmus was a close friend), St. Thomas More was executed on July 6, 1535, by King Henry VIII for refusing to sign the oath accepting Henry as the Supreme Head of the Church in England—an oath that was signed by all English bishops except one. In the following excerpt from *The Sadness of Christ*, a commentary on Christ's betrayal in the garden of Gethsemane that More wrote while a prisoner in the Tower of London, he warns against worldly corruption among the Church's bishops. Even while warning against corruption, he accepts their authority as ordained by Christ.

SEE NOW, WHEN CHRIST comes back to His apostles for the third time, there they are, buried in sleep, though He commanded them to bear up with Him and to stay awake and pray because of the impending danger; but Judas the traitor at the same time was so wide awake and intent on betraying the Lord that the very idea of sleep never entered his mind.

Does not this contrast between the traitor and the apostles present to us a clear and sharp mirror image (as it were), a sad and terrible view

From: *The Sadness of Christ*, trans. Clarence Miller (New Haven, Conn.: Yale University Press, 1993), 46–50.

of what has happened through the ages from those times even to our own? Why do not bishops contemplate in this scene their own somnolence? Since they have succeeded in the place of the apostles, would that they would reproduce their virtues just as eagerly as they embrace their authority and as faithfully as they display their sloth and sleepiness! For very many are sleepy and apathetic in sowing virtues among the people and maintaining the truth, while the enemies of Christ, in order to sow vices and uproot the faith (that is, insofar as they can, to seize Christ and cruelly crucify Him once again), are wide awake—so much wiser (as Christ says) are the sons of darkness in their generation than the sons of light.

But although this comparison of the sleeping apostles applies very well to those bishops who sleep while virtue and the faith are placed in jeopardy, still it does not apply to all such prelates at all points. For some of them—alas, far more than I could wish—do not drift into sleep through sadness and grief as the apostles did. Rather, they are numbed and buried in destructive desires; that is, drunk with the new wine of the devil, the flesh, and the world, they sleep like pigs sprawling in the mire. Certainly the apostles' feeling of sadness because of the danger to their Master was praiseworthy, but for them to be so overcome by sadness as to yield completely to sleep, that was certainly wrong. Even to grieve because the world is perishing or to weep because of the crimes of others bespeaks a reverent outlook, as was felt by the writer who said, "I sat by myself and groaned" (Lam. 3:28) and also by the one who said, "I was sick at heart because of sinners abandoning your law" (Ps. 119:53). Sadness of this sort I would place in the category of which he says, "For the sorrow that is according to God produces repentance that surely tends to salvation, whereas the sorrow that is according to the world produces death" (2 Cor. 7:10). But I would place it there only if the feeling, however good, is checked by the rule and guidance of reason. For if this is not the case, if sorrow so grips the mind that its strength is sapped and reason gives up the reins, if a bishop is so overcome by heavy-hearted sleep that he neglects to do what the duty of his office requires for salvation of his flock—like a cowardly ship's captain who is so disheartened by the furious din of a storm that he deserts the helm, hides away cowering in some cranny, and abandons the ship to the waves—if a bishop does this, I would certainly not hesitate to juxtapose and compare his sadness with the sadness that leads, as [Paul] says, to hell; indeed, I would consider it far worse, since such sadness in religious matters seems to spring from a mind which despairs of God's help.

The next category, but a far worse one, consists of those who are not depressed by sadness at the danger of others but rather by a fear of injury to themselves, a fear which is so much the worse as its cause is the more contemptible, that is, when it is not a question of life or death but of money.

And yet Christ commands us to contemn the loss of the body itself for His sake. "Do not be afraid," He says, "of those who destroy the body and after that can do nothing further. But I will show you the one you should fear, the one to fear: fear Him who, when He has destroyed the body, has the power to send the soul also to hell. This, I tell you, is the one you must fear."

And though He lays down this rule for everyone without exception when they have been seized and there is no way out, He attaches a separate charge over and above this to the high office of prelates: He does not allow them to be concerned only about their own souls or merely to take refuge in silence until they are dragged out and forced to choose between open profession or lying dissimulation, but He also wished them to come forth if they see that the flock entrusted to them is in danger and to face the danger of their own accord for the good of their flock. "The good shepherd," says Christ, "lays down his life for his sheep." But if every good shepherd lays down his life for his sheep, certainly one who saves his own life to the detriment of his sheep is not fulfilling the role of a good shepherd.

Therefore, just as one who loses his life for Christ (and he does this if he loses it for the flock of Christ entrusted to him) saves it for life everlasting, so too one who denies Christ (and this he does if he fails to profess the truth when his silence injures his flock) by saving his life, he actually proceeds to lose it. Clearly it is even worse if, driven by fear, he denies Christ openly in words and forsakes Him publicly. Such prelates do not sleep like Peter, they make his waking denial. But under the kindly glance of Christ, most of them through His grace will eventually wipe out that failure and save themselves by weeping, if only they respond to His glance and friendly call to repentance with bitterness of heart and a new way of life, remembering His words and contemplating His passion and leaving behind the shackles of evil which bound them in their sins.

But if anyone is so set in evil that he does not merely neglect to profess the truth out of fear but like Arius and his ilk preaches false doctrine, whether for sordid gain or out of a corrupt ambition, such a person does not sleep like Peter, does not make Peter's denial, but rather stays awake with wicked Judas and like Judas persecutes Christ. This man's condition is far more dangerous than that of the others, as is shown by the sad and horrible end Judas came to. But since there is no limit to the kindness of a merciful God, even this sort of sinner ought not to despair of forgiveness. Even to Judas God gave many opportunities of coming to his senses. He did not deny him His companionship. He did not take away from him the dignity of his apostleship. He did not even take the purse-strings from him, even though he was a thief. He admitted the traitor to the fellowship of His beloved disciples at the Last Supper. He deigned to stoop down at the feet of the betrayer and to wash with His innocent and most sacred hands Judas' dirty feet, a most fit symbol of his filthy mind. Moreover, with incomparable generosity He gave him to eat, in the form of bread, that very body of His which the betrayer had already sold; and under the appearance of wine, He gave him that very blood to drink which, even while he was drinking it, the traitor was wickedly scheming to broach and set flowing. Finally, when Judas, coming with his crew to seize Him, offered Him a kiss, a kiss that was in fact the terrible token of his treachery, Christ received him calmly and gently. Who would not believe that any one of all these could have turned the traitor's mind, however hardened in crime, to better courses? Then too, even that beginning of repentance, when he admitted he had sinned and gave back the pieces of silver and threw them away when they were not accepted, crying out that he was a traitor and confessing that he had betrayed innocent blood—I am inclined to believe that Christ prompted him thus far so that He might if possible (that is, if the traitor did not add despair to his treachery) save from ruin the very man who had so recently, so perfidiously, betrayed Him to death.

Therefore, since God showed His great mercy in so many ways even toward Judas, an apostle turned traitor, since He invited him to forgiveness so often and did not allow him to perish except through despair alone, certainly there is no reason why, in this life, anyone should despair of any imitator of Judas. Rather, according to that holy advice of the apostle, "Pray for each other that you may be saved" (James 5:16), if we see anyone wandering wildly from the right road, let us hope that he will one day return to the path, and meanwhile let us pray humbly and incessantly that God will hold out to him chances to come to his senses, and likewise that with God's help he will eagerly seize them, and having seized them will hold fast and not throw them away out of malice or let them slip away from him through wretched sloth.

Questions for Thomas More

1. How does More compare the sleepiness of the apostles to the condition of the bishops (in England) in his own day?
2. What are the main faults of the bishops, according to More?
3. Rather than condemning the bishops as a lost cause, why does More emphasize that negligent bishops may still repent?

St. Jane de Chantal

Born into a prominent family, St. Jane de Chantal (1572–1641) married Baron Christophe de Rabutin-Chantal in 1592, and they had six children before his early death in a hunting accident. A few years later, in 1604, she met St. Francis de Sales, Bishop of Geneva. In 1610, the two co-founded the Visitation of Holy Mary in Annecy, and St. Jane de Chantal devoted the rest of her life to building up this religious community in accord with what came to be known as Salesian spirituality. I have selected some letters of spiritual direction that St. Jane de Chantal sent to her brother André Frémyot, the Archbishop of Bourges. Her letters emphasize the need for continual prayer.

Chambery, 1625
My very dear Lord,

SINCE GOD, IN HIS eternal goodness, has moved you to consecrate all your love, your actions, your works, and your whole self to Him utterly without any self-interest but only for His greater glory and His satisfaction, remain firm in this resolve. With the confidence of a son, rest in the care and love which divine Providence has for you in all your needs. Look upon Providence as a child does its mother who loves him

Excerpts *from* "Letters of Spiritual Direction," *Francis de Sales and Jane de Chantal, Letters of Spiritual Direction,* trans. Péronne Marie Thibert, Classics of Western Spirituality Series, copyright © 1988, 201–206. Used with permission of Paulist Press, *www.paulistpress.com.*

tenderly. You can be sure that God loves you incomparably more. We can't imagine how great is the love which God, in His goodness, has for souls who thus abandon themselves to His mercy, and who have no other wish than to do what they think pleases Him, leaving everything that concerns them to His care in time and in eternity.

After this, every day in your morning exercise, or at the end of it, confirm your resolutions and unite your will with God's in all that you will do that day and in whatever He sends you. Use words like these: "O most holy Will of God, I give You infinite thanks for the mercy with which You have surrounded me; with all my strength and love, I adore You from the depths of my soul and unite my will to Yours now and forever, especially in all that I shall do and all that You will be pleased to send me this day, consecrating to Your glory my soul, my mind, my body, all my thoughts, words and actions, and my whole being. I beg You, with all the humility of my heart, accomplish in me Your eternal designs, and do not allow me to present any obstacle to this. Your eyes, which can see the most intimate recesses of my heart, know the intensity of my desire to live out Your holy will, but they can also see my weakness and limitations. That is why, prostrate before Your infinite mercy, I implore You, my Savior, through the gentleness and justice of this same will of Yours, to grant me the grace of accomplishing it perfectly, so that, consumed in the fire of Your love, I may be an acceptable holocaust which, with the glorious Virgin and all the saints, will praise and bless You forever. Amen."

During the activities of the day, spiritual as well as temporal, as often as you can, my dear Lord, unite your will to God's by confirming your morning resolution. Do this either by a simple, loving glance at God, or by a few words spoken quietly and cast into His heart, by assenting in words like: "Yes, Lord, I want to do this action because You want it," or simply, "Yes, Father," or, "O Holy Will, live and rule in me," or other words that the Holy Spirit will suggest to you. You may also make a simple sign of the cross over your heart, or kiss the cross you are wearing. All this will show that above everything, you want to do the holy will of God and seek nothing but His glory in all that you do.

As for the will of God's good pleasure, which we know only through events as they occur, if these events benefit us, we must bless God and unite ourselves to this divine will which sends them. If something occurs which is disagreeable, physically or mentally, let us lovingly unite our will in obedience to the divine good pleasure, despite our natural aversion. We must pay no attention to these feelings, so long as at the fine point of our will we acquiesce very simply to God's will, saying, "O my God, I want this because it is Your good pleasure." Chapter 6 of Book IX of the *Love of God* throws a clear light on this practice and invites us to be courageous and simple in performing it. Whatever good or evil befalls you, be confident that God will convert it all to your good.

As for prayer, don't burden yourself with making considerations; neither your mind nor mine is good at that. Follow your own way of speaking to our Lord sincerely, lovingly, confidently, and simply, as your heart dictates. Sometimes be content to stay ever so short a while in His divine presence, faithfully and humbly, like a child before his father, waiting to be told what to do, totally dependent on the paternal will in which he has placed all his love and trust. You may, if you wish, say a few words on this subject, but very quietly: "You are my Father and my God from whom I expect all my happiness." A few moments later (for you must always wait a little to hear what God will say to your heart): "I am Your child, all Yours; good children think only of pleasing their father; I don't want to have any worries and I leave in Your care everything that concerns me, for You love me, my God. Father, You are my good. My soul rests and trusts in Your love and eternal providence." Try to let yourself be penetrated by words like these.

When you have committed some fault, go to God humbly, saying to Him, "I have sinned, my God, and I am sorry." Then, with loving confidence, add: "Father, pour the oil of Your bountiful mercy on my wounds, for You are my only hope; heal me." A little later: "By the help of Your grace, I shall be more on my guard and will bless you eternally," and speak like this according to the different movements and feelings of your soul. Sometimes put yourself very simply before God, certain of His presence everywhere, and without any effort, whisper very softly to His sacred heart whatever your own heart prompts you to say.

When you are experiencing some physical pain or a sorrowful heart, try to endure it before God, recalling as much as you can that He is watching you at this time of affliction, especially in physical illness when very often the heart is weary and unable to pray. Don't force yourself to pray, for a simple adherence to God's will, expressed from time to time, is enough. Moreover, suffering borne in the will quietly and patiently is a continual, very powerful prayer before God, regardless of the complaints and anxieties that come from the inferior part of the soul.

Finally, my dear Lord, try to perform all your actions calmly and gently, and keep your mind every joyful, peaceful, and content. Do not worry about your perfection, or about your soul. God to whom it belongs, and to whom you have completely entrusted it, will take care of it and fill it with all the graces, consolations and blessings of His holy love in the measure that they will be useful in this life. In the next life He will grant you eternal bliss. Such is the wish of her to whom your soul is as precious as her own; pray for her, for she never prays without you, my Lord.

Annecy, 8 May 1625
My very honored and beloved Lord,

May the divine Savior, who ascends, glorious and triumphant, to sit at the right hand of His Father, draw to Himself our hearts and all our affections, in order to place them in the bosom of His love! How consoled I was when I read your letter and saw the graces and mercy that this good Savior has granted you! I have blessed Him and thanked Him for this; I do so again with all my heart, and I shall continue to thank Him unceasingly.

It is good when a soul loves solitude; it's a sign that it takes delight in God and enjoys speaking with Him. Don't you see, my dearest Lord, this is where the divine sweetness communicates its lights and more abundant graces. How great is the grace you have received in this self-examination and the renewal of your soul which you have made with such preparation! Now you experience the fruit of this: peace and contentment in your conscience which is so well-prepared that God will be pleased to fill it with His most holy, precious favors. How strongly I feel about this and what great hope I have that it will lead you to utter integrity and perfection! You must respond faithfully to the lights that God will give you, no matter what it costs you, for really, the love which God, in His goodness, has for you, and which He manifests so openly by such excellent, solid graces, requires a reciprocal love, according to the measure of your weakness and poverty. This means that you must refuse nothing you recognize to be His will. This perfect abandonment of yourself in the arms of divine Providence, this loving acceptance of all that He wishes to do with you, and with everything, this peace of conscience, this holy desire to please Him by all kinds of virtuous acts, according to the opportunities He will give you, and especially acts of charity and humility—all this is the wood that will feed the fire of sacred love which you feel in your heart and continually desire. And in this holy exercise, do not forget me, my very dear Lord, so that some day—God knows when—we may see each other in that blessed eternity where we shall love Him and praise and bless Him with all our strength. . . .

Pont-à-Mousson, 1 June 1626
My very dear and honored Lord,

I thank and praise our good God for the blessing He is pleased to have given us through the exchange made possible by our perfect friendship; for I assure you that if my letters enkindle in you the flame of love for the supreme Good, your very dear letters arouse the same feelings in me and make me wish more and more that our hearts be totally and constantly united to the good pleasure of God which we find so kind and favorable. Let us love this good pleasure, my dearest Lord, and let us see it alone in all that happens to us, embracing it lovingly. May this exercise be our daily bread. It can be practiced everywhere, and is particularly necessary for you because of the variety of obligations and contracts which you cannot avoid; for, in everything, by God's grace, you seek only Him and His most holy will.

Oh! how satisfying it is to read and reread what you tell me, my very dear Lord—of how you continue to practice your spiritual exercises with the same fervor and love you had when you began them, and how you keep your resolutions vigorous, despite the bustle of the court.

Confident of the Lord's goodness, I trust you will never retreat but will continually advance. Your assurance and testimony about this give my soul consolation and peace. That's why I beg you, my dearest Lord, always to mention something on this subject when you write to me. And don't think that this desire comes from mistrust, certainly not. I have no fear of that, now that your year of "novitiate" is over; and I have never doubted that God would grant you a holy perseverance, for the grace of your vocation in the service of His pure love is too extraordinary and abundant. Let us both appreciate and love this grace well, my very dear Lord, since it is the source of eternal life for us. It is so precious to me that I rank it second among all the God-given graces which impel me most strongly to do good and to long to see our life totally bound with Jesus Christ and hidden in God.

Do not think that by this I mean for us to retire into solitude, or to flee those occupations and legitimate contacts necessary to our vocations; oh, no, for I very much like each one to stay in his state of life and not throw himself into the excesses of a hermit's devotion, especially you, my dearest Lord, for whom this would be most inappropriate. But what I do mean is that we must want, above all, to adorn our souls with the virtues of our Savior, Jesus Christ, and also with that secret, intimate union of our hearts with God, which causes us to long for Him everywhere, as you are doing. As for that humility of heart which makes you think of yourself as a blade of hyssop in comparison to her whom you consider a cedar of Lebanon—though, in truth, she is but a shadow and lifeless image of virtue—my dear Lord, this is the humility which attracts God's Spirit to our souls and fills them with the treasure of all virtues. It is through humility that we live a hidden life, for she manages her good works in secret and holds in security, in the shelter of her protection, the little good that we do.

I didn't intend to write so much, dearest Lord, but that's how my heart always opens up to you. And certainly it is very softened by the holy and incomparable love God has given it for you. Always love this heart of mine well and continue to recommend it to the divine mercy. Be assured that I never cease desiring for you the fullness of His best graces in this life and a very high place before the throne of His glory and only desirable eternity. But all this, no doubt, I do with infinite love and affection.

Questions for Jane de Chantal

1. How does Jane urge the Archbishop to pray? Why does she urge him to focus on God's will rather than his own?
2. In what way is the Archbishop to be like a child?
3. Why is abandonment to divine Providence required?

Jean-Jacques Olier

Jean-Jacques Olier (1608–1657) belonged, along with Cardinal Pierre de Bérulle and John Eudes, to what is now known as "the French School" of seventeenth-century Catholic spirituality. A priest influenced by the thought of Bérulle, Jean-Jacques Olier was the leading founder of a religious order, the Sulpicians (the Society of St. Sulpice, named for the parish where Olier was pastor). With his Sulpician companions, Olier founded a number of seminaries throughout France in order to renew and reform the priesthood. In the following selection from his writings, Olier urges priests—as creatures, sinners, Christians, and priests—to model the virtue of patience, because it is in this way that priests can fully endure all sufferings with Christ. The dignity of the priesthood, according to Olier, consists in this vocation to suffer humbly the humiliations that Christ suffered.

W E ARE OBLIGED TO BE patient. First, in our condition as creatures; for God, sovereign master of life and death, on whom our existence depends absolutely, has the right to dispose of us as he chooses.

Saint Paul says that the potter has the right to do whatever he wishes with his pot (Rom. 9:21) since it is the work of his hands. He shatters it,

Excerpted *from* "Introduction to the Christian Life and Virtues," ed. William Thompson, *Bérulle and the French School,* trans. Lowell M. Glendon, Classics of Western Spirituality Series, copyright © 1989, 244–247. Used with permission of Paulist Press, *www.paulistpress.com.*

he breaks it, he refashions it, he molds it, he bends it, he compresses it and shapes it as he wills.

This is how we are in the hands of God. Since we are the work of his hands, he can do with us anything he wishes. Whether he shatters, breaks, kills, mortifies, plunges us to the depth of hell and takes us out again, this is totally in his hands and we should suffer it in peace, adoring his desires, his judgments and his designs for his handiwork and remaining completely abandoned to his good pleasure.

Second, as sinners. For in this condition, we must bear with the effects of his justice and wrath toward us. All the punishments that he carries out in this world are nothing compared with what we deserve and what he would make us suffer if he did not choose to be merciful toward us and to treat us with gentleness and clemency in this life.

The punishments that God meted out to sinners, as we see in the holy scripture, even the torments of the damned and the penalties the demons suffer and will suffer eternally for one sin, should cause us not only to be at peace, but to rejoice in our sufferings.

In fact, what is there in hell that we do not deserve? What torments do they suffer there that we do not merit as well and a thousand times more? For mercy is even found in hell and we are not worthy of it. Should not this insight compel us to bear patiently all the difficulties and tribulations of this life, especially since our Lord says that these are signs of his love? "I reprove and I chastise those whom I love" (Rev. 3:19).

Third, as Christians. For as such we should bear with many difficulties and sufferings. This is why we are initiated into the church. For our Lord only admitted us into it to continue his life, which is a life of opposition, contradiction, and condemnation toward the flesh.

He must then humiliate it and subdue it in us, using the ways he knows and judges to be most useful, so as to win a complete victory. He first achieved victory in his own flesh, and he wishes to continue it in ours in order to show forth in us a sample of the universal triumph that he had achieved over it in his own person.

The church and Christians are only a handful of flesh compared to the whole world. Nevertheless, he still desires to be victorious in them to proclaim his triumph and to give definite signs of his victory. Thus, from this perspective, the Christian should be very faithful to the Spirit and completely abandoned to him in order to overcome the flesh and to destroy it completely.

There will be no lack of opportunities in this life, for he must suffer: first, the attacks of the world through scorn, calumny, and persecution; second, the violent onslaughts of the flesh in its uprisings and its revolts; third, the battles with the devil in the temptations he sends us; finally, the ordeals from God through dryness, desolation, abandonment, and other interior difficulties, which he afflicts on him in order to initiate him into the perfect crucifixion of the flesh.

Fourth, as clerics. For clerics should participate in the fulfillment of Christianity. This cannot exist without patience.

Patience is a sign that the soul is intimately united to God and that it is rooted in perfection. For it must be very much in God and fully possessed by him in order to bear difficulties and torments with peace, tranquillity, and even joy and beatitude in one's heart.

It must be quite profoundly immersed in him and remain quite powerfully and strongly united to him, so that the flesh has no power at all to attract it to itself and share with him the feelings and aversions that it has toward suffering and endurance.

In this state the soul experiences the perfection attainable in this life, since it conforms to our Lord's perfect submission to God during his sufferings. For although his flesh experienced aversion and revulsion for the cross, he paid no attention to it with his will. Rather, he always adhered perfectly to the wishes of his Father.

Therefore clerics, being perfect Christians chosen from the midst of the church to assist before the tabernacle of God, should pay particular attention to this virtue. This is their very nature. It is the sign by which they can be identified. This is what predisposes them for the honorable rank that they possess. This is how they are recognized as domestics and servants of God.

Finally, priests and pastors should have a very high degree of patience because, in Jesus Christ and with Jesus Christ, they are both priests and victims for the sins of the world. Jesus Christ the priest wished to be the victim of his sacrifice. He became the host-victim for all people. Since priests are like sacraments and representations of him who lives in them to continue his priesthood and whom he clothes with his external conduct and his interior dispositions, as well as with his power and his person, he wishes furthermore that they be interiorly rooted in the spirit and dispositions of a host-victim in order to suffer, endure, do penance, in short, to immolate themselves for the glory of God and the salvation of the people.

In imitation of our Lord, priests should not only be victims for sin through persecution, penance, internal and external sufferings, but also they should be like the victims of a holocaust. This is their true vocation. For they should not merely suffer, as he did, all sorts of difficulties both for their own sins and the sins of the people entrusted to them, but even more they should be entirely consumed with him through love.

The spirit of love strengthens and empowers us to endure affliction and suffering, no matter how great they are. Since he is infinite, he gives us as much as we need to endure those that can occur in our vocation.

All the torments of the world are nothing to a generous soul filled with the power of God, who is able to shoulder countless sufferings more violent than all those that the world and the devil might afflict us with. It is with this Spirit that Saint Paul said: "I can do all things in him who strengthens me" (Phil. 4:13). Everything he saw seemed little to do or suffer because of the God who dwelled in him.

It is through this same eternal, immense and all-powerful Spirit that he called his sufferings light and momentary, because Jesus Christ who suffered and bore them in himself and allowed him to see and experience something of his eternity through his presence, caused him to look upon the entire duration of this life as but a moment. This is how our Lord, who allows us to experience interiorly that his power and strength could support a thousand worlds, leads us to call his burden light.

However, it is not as if he does not occasionally withdraw his tangible strength from us so that we might experience the burden of tribulation in the weakness of our flesh and in the frailty to which it is reduced because of his absence. However, he makes us endure this abandonment in order to produce two wonderful effects in our souls.

The first is to mistrust ourselves and the weaknesses of the flesh. The second is to appreciate God and his strength. For in this state we are necessarily forced to turn to God and to dwell in him so that we might be strengthened and sustained in order to accomplish and to suffer all that he wishes for his glory.

Questions for Olier

1. Describe how Olier calls upon priests to bear difficulties patiently, rather than becoming angry at or disillusioned with God.

2. What does Olier identify as the sufferings that the believer will undergo?
3. Why is patience such an important virtue? How does patience enable priests to imitate Christ and rely upon God's strength, given by the Holy Spirit?

John Henry Newman

John Henry Newman (1801–1890) converted to Catholicism from
Anglicanism in 1845. The greatest theologian of the 19th century,
Newman is best known for his theory of the development of doc-
trine, but his work spanned a wide range of important themes. His
Apologia Pro Vita Sua, explaining his conversion, is today recognized
as a literary classic. Famous as an Anglican priest for his sermons,
Newman joined the Oratory of St. Philip Neri when he became a
Catholic, and *Discourses Addressed to Mixed Congregations*, a collec-
tion of sermons, was his first published work written as a Catholic.
In the third discourse, "Men, Not Angels, the Priests of the Gospel,"
reprinted in full below, Newman reflects upon the simultaneous
dignity and unworthiness of priests.

WHEN CHRIST, THE GREAT Prophet, the great Preacher, the great Missionary, came into the world, He came in a way the most holy, the
most august, the most glorious. Though He came in humiliation,
though He came to suffer, though He was born in a stable, though He
was laid in a manger, yet He issued from the womb of an Immaculate
Mother, and His infant form shone with heavenly light. Sanctity marked
every lineament of His character and every circumstance of His mission.

*From: John Henry Cardinal Newman, Discourses Addressed to Mixed Congrega-
tions*, Discourse III (New York: Longmans, Green, 1916), 43–61.

Gabriel announced His incarnation; a Virgin conceived, a Virgin bore, a Virgin suckled Him; His foster-father was the pure and saintly Joseph; Angels proclaimed His birth; a luminous star spread the news among the heathen; the austere Baptist went before His face; and a crowd of shriven penitents, clad in white garments and radiant with grace, followed Him wherever He went. As the sun in heaven shines through the clouds, and is reflected in the landscape, so the eternal Sun of justice, when He rose upon the earth, turned night into day, and in His brightness made all things bright.

He came and He went; and, seeing that He came to introduce a new and final Dispensation into the world, He left behind Him preachers, teachers, and missionaries, in His stead. Well then, my brethren, you will say, since on His coming all about Him was so glorious, such as He was, such must His servants be, such His representatives, His ministers, in His absence; as He was without sin, they too must be without sin; as He was the Son of God, they must surely be Angels. Angels, you will say, must be appointed to this high office; Angels alone are fit to preach the birth, the sufferings, the death of God. They might indeed have to hide their brightness, as He before them, their Lord and Master, had put on a disguise; they might come, as they came under the Old Covenant, in the garb of men; but still men they could not be, if they were to be preachers of the everlasting Gospel, and dispensers of its divine mysteries. If they were to sacrifice, as He had sacrificed; to continue, repeat, apply, the very Sacrifice which He had offered; to take into their hands that very Victim which was He Himself; to bind and to loose, to bless and to ban, to receive the confessions of His people, and to give them absolution for their sins; to teach them the way of truth, and to guide them along the way of peace; who was sufficient for these things but an inhabitant of those blessed realms of which the Lord is the never-failing Light?

And yet, my brethren, so it is, He has sent forth for the ministry of reconciliation, not Angels, but men; He has sent forth your brethren to you, not beings of some unknown nature and some strange blood, but of your own bone and your own flesh, to preach to you. "Ye men of Galilee, why stand ye gazing up into heaven?" Here is the royal style and tone in which Angels speak to men, even though these men be Apostles; it is the tone of those who, having never sinned, speak from their lofty eminence to those who have. But such is not the tone of those whom Christ has sent; for it is your brethren whom He has appointed, and none else—sons of Adam, sons of your nature, the same by nature, differing only in grace—men, like you, exposed to temptations, to the same temptations, to the same warfare within and without; with the same three deadly enemies—the world, the flesh, and the devil; with the same human, the same wayward heart: differing only as the power of God has changed and rules it. So it is; we are not Angels from Heaven that speak to you, but men, whom grace, and grace alone, has made to differ from you. Listen to the Apostle: When the barbarous Lycaonians, seeing his miracle, would have sacrificed to him and St. Barnabas, as to gods, he rushed in among them, crying out, "O men, why do ye this? We also are mortals, men like unto you"; or, as the words run more forcibly in the original Greek, "We are of like passions with you." And again to the Corinthians he writes, "We preach not ourselves, but Jesus Christ our Lord; and ourselves your servants through Jesus. God, who commanded the light to shine out of darkness, He hath shined in our hearts, to give the light of the knowledge of the glory of God in the face of Christ Jesus: *but* we hold this treasure *in earthen vessels.*" And further, he says of himself most wonderfully, that, "lest he should be exalted by the greatness of the revelations," there was given him "an angel of Satan" in his flesh "to buffet him." Such are your Ministers, your Preachers, your Priests, O my brethren; not Angels, not Saints, not sinless, but those who would have lived and died in sin except for God's grace, and who, though through God's mercy they be in training for the fellowship of Saints hereafter, yet at present are in the midst of infirmity and temptation, and have no hope, except from the unmerited grace of God, of persevering unto the end.

What a strange, what a striking anomaly is this! All is perfect, all is heavenly, all is glorious, in the Dispensation which Christ has vouchsafed us, except the persons of His Ministers. He dwells on our altars Himself, the Most Holy, the Most High, in light inaccessible, and Angels fall down before Him there; and out of visible substances and forms He chooses what is choicest to represent and to hold Him. The finest wheat-flour, and the purest wine, are taken as His outward symbols; the most sacred and majestic words minister to the sacrificial rite; altar and sanctuary are adorned decently or splendidly, as our means allow; and the Priests perform their office in befitting vestments, lifting up chaste hearts and holy hands; yet those very Priests, so set apart, so consecrated, they, with their girdle of celibacy and their

maniple of sorrow, are sons of Adam, sons of sinners, of a fallen nature, which they have not put off, though it be renewed through grace,
so that it is almost the definition of a Priest that he has sins of his own
to offer for. "Every high Priest," says the Apostle, "taken from among
men, is appointed for men, in the things that appertain unto God, that
he may offer gifts and sacrifices for sins; who can condole with those
who are in ignorance and error, because he also himself is compassed
with infirmity. And therefore he ought, as for the people, so also for
himself, to offer for sins." And hence in the Mass, when he offers up
the Host before consecration, he says, *Suscipe, Sancte Pater, Om-
nipotens, aeterne Deus,* "Accept, Holy Father, Almighty, Everlasting
God, this immaculate Host, which I, Thine unworthy servant, offer to
Thee, my Living and True God, for *mine* innumerable sins, offences,
and negligences, *and* for all who stand around, and for all faithful
Christians, living and dead."

Most strange is this in itself, my brethren, but not strange, when you
consider it is the appointment of an all-merciful God; not strange in
Him, because the Apostle gives the reason of it in the passage I have
quoted. The priests of the New Law are men, in order that they may
"condole with those who are in ignorance and error, because they too
are compassed with infirmity." Had Angels been your Priests, my
brethren, they could not have condoled with you, sympathized with you,
have had compassion on you, felt tenderly for you, and made allowances
for you, as we can; they could not have been your patterns and guides,
and have led you on from your old selves into a new life, as they can who
come from the midst of you, who have been led on themselves as you are
to be led, who know well your difficulties, who have had experience, at
least of your temptations, who know the strength of the flesh and the
wiles of the devil, even though they have baffled them, who are already
disposed to take your part, and be indulgent towards you, and can advise you most practically, and warn you most seasonably and prudently.
Therefore did He send you men to be the ministers of reconciliation and
intercession; as He Himself, though He could not sin, yet even He, by becoming man, took on Him, as far as was possible to God, man's burden
of infirmity and trial in His own person. He could not be a sinner, but
He could be a man, and He took to Himself a man's heart that we might
entrust our hearts to Him, and "was tempted in all things, like as we are,
yet without sin."

Ponder this truth well, my brethren, and let it be your comfort. Among the Preachers, among the Priests of the Gospel, there have been Apostles, there have been Martyrs, there have been Doctors—Saints in plenty among them; yet out of them all, high as has been their sanctity, varied their graces, awful their gifts, there has not been one who did not begin with the old Adam; not one of them who was not hewn out of the same rock as the most obdurate of reprobates; not one of them who was not fashioned unto honour out of the same clay which has been the material of the most polluted and vile of sinners; not one who was not by nature brother of those poor souls who have now commenced an eternal fellowship with the devil, and are lost in hell. Grace has vanquished nature; that is the whole history of the Saints. Salutary thought for those who are tempted to pride themselves in what they do, and what they are; wonderful news for those who sorrowfully recognise in their hearts the vast difference that exists between them and the Saints; and joyful news, when men hate sin, and wish to escape from its miserable yoke, yet are tempted to think it impossible!

Come, my brethren, let us look at this truth more narrowly, and lay it to heart. First consider, that, since Adam fell, none of his seed but has been conceived in sin; none, save one. One exception there has been— who is that one? Not our Lord Jesus, for He was not conceived of man, but of the Holy Ghost; not our Lord, but I mean His Virgin Mother, who, though conceived and born of human parents, as others, yet was rescued by anticipation from the common condition of mankind, and never was partaker in fact of Adam's transgression. She was conceived in the way of nature, she was conceived as others are; but grace interfered and was beforehand with sin; grace filled her soul from the first moment of her existence, so that the evil one breathed not on her, nor stained with work of God. *Tota pulchra es, Maria; et macula originalis non est in te.* "Thou art all fair, O Mary, and the stain original is not in thee." But putting aside the Most Blessed Mother of God, every one else, the most glorious Saint, and the most black and odious of sinners, I mean, the soul which, in the event, became the most glorious, and the soul which became the most devilish, were both born in one and the same original sin, both were children of wrath, both were unable to attain heaven by their natural powers, both had the prospect of meriting for themselves hell.

They were both born in sin; they both lay in sin; and the soul, which afterwards became a Saint, would have continued in sin, would have sinned willfully, and would have been lost, but for the visitings of an un-merited supernatural influence upon it, which did for it what it could not do for itself. The poor infant, destined to be an heir of glory, lay fee-ble, sickly, fretful, wayward, and miserable; the child of sorrow; without hope, and without heavenly aid. So it lay for many a long and weary day ere it was born; and when at length it opened its eyes and saw the light, it shrank back, and wept aloud that it had seen it. But God heard its cry from heaven in this valley of tears, and He began that course of mercies towards it which led it from earth to heaven. He sent His Priest to ad-minister to it the first sacrament, and to baptise it with His grace. Then a great change took place in it, for, instead of its being any more the thrall of Satan it forthwith became a child of God; and had it died that minute, and before it came to the age of reason, it would have been car-ried to heaven without delay by Angels, and been admitted into the pres-ence of God.

But it did not die; it came to the age of reason, and, oh, shall we dare to say, though in some blessed cases it may be said, shall we dare to say, that it did not misuse the great talent which had been given to it, pro-fane the grace which dwelt in it, and fall into mortal sin? In some in-stances, praised be God! we dare affirm it; such seems to have been the case with my own dear father, St. Phillip, who surely kept his baptismal robe unsullied from the day he was clad in it, never lost his state of grace from the day he was put into it, and proceeded from strength to strength, and from merit to merit, and from glory to glory, through the whole course of his long life, till at the age of eighty he was summoned to his account, and went joyfully to meet it, and was carried across pur-gatory, without any scorching of its flames, straight to heaven.

Such certainly have sometimes been the dealings of God's grace with the souls of His elect; but more commonly, as if more intimately to as-sociate them with their brethren, and to make the fullness of His favours to them a ground of hope and an encouragement to the penitent sinner, those who have ended in being miracles of sanctity, and heroes in the Church, have passed a time in willful disobedience, have thrown them-selves out of the light of God's countenance, have been led captive by this or that sin, by this or that religious error, till at length they were in various ways recovered, slowly or suddenly, and regained the state of grace or rather a much higher state, than that which they had forfeited. Such was the blessed Magdalen, who had lived a life of shame; so much

so, that even to be touched by her was, according to the religious judgment of her day, a pollution. Happy in this world's goods, young and
passionate, she had given her heart to the creature, before the grace of
God prevailed with her. Then she cut off her long hair, and put aside her
gay apparel, and became so utterly what she had not been, that, had you
known her before and after, you would have said it was two persons you
had seen, not one; for there was no trace of the sinner in the penitent,
except the affectionate heart, now set on heaven and Christ; no trace be-
sides, no memory of that glittering and seductive apparition, in the
modest form, the serene countenance, the composed gait, and the gentle voice of her who in the garden sought and found her Risen Saviour.
Such, too, was he who from a publican became an Apostle and an Evangelist; one who for filthy lucre scrupled not to enter the service of the
heathen Romans, and to oppress his own people. Nor were the rest of
the Apostles made of better clay than the other sons of Adam; they were
by nature animal, carnal, ignorant; left to themselves, they would, like
the brutes, have groveled on the earth, and gazed upon the earth, and fed
on the earth, had not the grace of God taken possession of them, and set
them on their feet, and raised their faces heavenward. And such was the
learned Pharisee, who came to Jesus by night, well satisfied with his sta-
tion, jealous of his reputation, confident in his reason; but the time at
length came, when, even though disciples fled, he remained to anoint
the abandoned corpse of Him, whom when living he had been ashamed
to own. You see it was the grace of God that triumphed in Magdalen, in
Matthew, and in Nicodemus; heavenly grace came down upon corrupt
nature; it subdued impurity in the youthful woman, covetousness in the
publican, fear of man in the Pharisee.

Let me speak of another celebrated conquest of God's grace in an after
age, and you will see how it pleases Him to make a Confessor, a Saint and
Doctor of His Church, out of sin and heresy both together. It was not
enough that the Father of the Western Schools, the author of a thousand
works, the triumphant controversialist, the especial champion of grace,
should have been once a poor slave of the flesh, but he was the victim of
a perverted intellect also. He, who of all others, was to extol the grace of
God, was left more than others to experience the helplessness of nature.
The great St. Augustine—I am not speaking of the holy missionary of
the same name, who came to England and converted our pagan forefa-
thers, and became the first Archbishop of Canterbury, but of the great

African Bishop, two centuries before him—Augustine, I say, not being in earnest about his soul, not asking himself the question, how was sin to be washed away, but rather being serious, while youth and strength lasted, to enjoy the flesh and the world, ambitious and sensual, judged of truth and falsehood by his private judgment and his private fancy; despised the Catholic Church because it spoke so much faith and subjection, thought to make his own reason the measure of all things, and accordingly joined a far-spread sect, which affected to be philosophical and enlightened, to take large views of things, and to correct the vulgar, that is the Catholic notions of God and Christ, of sin, and of the way to heaven. In this sect of his he remained for some years; yet what he was taught there did not satisfy him. It pleased him for a time, and then he found he had been eating as if food what had no nourishment in it; he became hungry and thirsty after something more substantial, he knew not what; he despised himself for being a slave to the flesh, and he found his religion did not help him to overcome it; thus he understood that he had not gained the truth, and he cried out, "O, who will tell me where to seek it, and who will bring me into it?"

Why did he not join the Catholic Church at once? I have told you why; he saw that truth was nowhere else; but he was not sure it was there. He thought there was something mean, narrow, irrational, in her system of doctrine; he lacked the gift of faith. Then a great conflict began within him—the conflict of nature with grace; of nature and her children, the flesh and false reason, against conscience and the pleadings of the Divine Spirit, leading him to better things. Though he was still in a state of perdition, yet God was visiting him, and giving him the first fruits of those influences which were in the event to bring him out of it. Time went on; and looking at him, as his Guardian Angel might look at him, you would have said that, in spite of much perverseness, and many a successful struggle against his Almighty Adversary, in spite of his still being, as before, in a state of wrath, nevertheless grace was making way in his soul—he was advancing towards the Church. He did not know it himself, he could not recognise it himself; but an eager interest in him, and then a joy, was springing up in heaven among the Angels of God. At last he came within the range of a great Saint in a foreign country; and, though he pretended not to acknowledge him, his attention was arrested by him, and he could not help coming to sacred places to look at him again and again. He began to watch him and speculate about him, and wondered with himself whether he was happy. He found himself frequently in Church, listening to the holy preacher, and he once asked his advice how to find what he was seeking. And now a final conflict came on him with the flesh: it was hard, very hard, to part with the indulgences of years, it was hard to part and never to meet again. O, sin was so sweet, how could he bid it farewell? How could he tear himself away from its embrace, and betake himself to that lonely and dreary way which led heavenwards? But God's grace was sweeter far, and it convinced him while it won him; it convinced his reason, and prevailed—and he who without it would have lived and died a child of Satan, became, under its wonderworking power, an oracle of sanctity and truth.

And do you not think, my brethren, that he was better fitted than another to persuade his brethren as he had been persuaded, and to preach the holy doctrine which he had despised? Not that sin is better than obedience, or the sinner than the just; but that God in His mercy makes use of sin against itself, that He turns past sin into a present benefit, that, while He washes away its guilt and subdues its power, He leaves it in the penitent in such sense as enables him, from his knowledge of its devices, to assault it more vigorously, and strike at it more truly, when it meets him in other men; that, while our Lord, by His omnipotent grace, can make the soul as clean as if it had never been unclean, He leaves it in possession of a tenderness and compassion for other sinners, an experience how to deal with them, greater than if it had never sinned; and again that, in those rare and special instances, of one of which I have been speaking, He holds up to us, for our instruction and our comfort, what He can do, even for the most guilty, if they sincerely come to Him for a pardon and a cure. There is no limit to be put to the bounty and power of God's grace; and that we feel sorrow for our sins, and supplicate His mercy, is a sort of present pledge to us in our hearts, that He will grant us the good gifts we are seeking. He can do what He will with the soul of man. He is infinitely more powerful than the foul spirit to whom the sinner has sold himself, and can cast him out.

O my dear brethren, though your conscience witnesses against you, He can disburden it; whether you have sinned less or whether you have sinned more, He can make you as clean in His sight and as acceptable to Him as if you had never gone from Him. Gradually will He destroy your sinful habits, and at once will He restore you to His favour. Such is the power of the Sacrament of Penance, that, be your load of guilt heavier or be it lighter, it removes it, whatever it is. It is as easy to Him to wash out the many sins as the few. Do you recollect in the Old Testament the history of the cure of Naaman the Syrian, by the prophet Eliseus? He had that dreadful, incurable disease called leprosy, which was a white crust upon the skin, making the whole person hideous, and typifying the hideousness of sin. The prophet bade him bathe in the river Jordan, and the disease disappeared; "his flesh," says the inspired writer, was "restored to him as the flesh of a little child." Here, then, we have a representation not only of what sin is, but of what God's grace is. It can undo the past, it can realise the hopeless. No sinner, ever so odious, but may become a Saint; no Saint, ever so exalted, but has been, or might have been, a sinner. Grace overcomes nature, and grace only overcomes it. Take that holy child, the blessed St. Agnes, who, at the age of thirteen, resolved to die rather than deny the faith, and stood enveloped in an atmosphere of purity, and diffused around her a heavenly influence, in the very home of evil spirits into which the heathen brought her; or consider the angelical Aloysius, of whom it hardly is left upon record that he committed even a venial sin; or St. Agatha, St. Juliana, St. Rose, St. Casimir, or St. Stanislas, to whom the very notion of any unbecoming imagination had been as death; well, there is not one of these seraphic souls but might have been a degraded, loathsome leper, except for God's grace, an outcast from his kind; not one but might, or rather would, have lived the life of a brute creature, and died the death of a reprobate, and lain down in hell eternally in the devil's arms, had not God put a new heart and a new spirit within him, and made him what he could not make himself.

All good men are not Saints, my brethren—all converted souls do not become Saints. I will not promise that, if you turn to God, you will reach that height of sanctity which the Saints have reached—true; still, I am showing you that even the Saints are by nature no better than you; and so (much more) that the Priests, who have the charge of the faithful, whatever be their sanctity, are by nature no better than those whom they have to convert, whom they have to reform. It is God's special mercy towards you that we by nature are no other than you; it is His consideration and compassion for you that He has made us, who are your brethren, His legates and ministers of reconciliation.

This is what the world cannot understand; not that it does not apprehend clearly enough that we are by nature of like passions with itself; but what it is so blind, so narrow-minded as not to comprehend, is, that, being so like itself by nature, we may be made so different by grace. Men of the world, my brethren, know the power of nature; they know not, experience not, believe not, the power of God's grace; and since they are not themselves acquainted with any power that can overcome nature, they think that none exists, and therefore, consistently, they believe that every one, Priest or not, remains to the end such as nature made him, and they will not believe it possible that any one can lead a supernatural life. Now, not Priest only, but every one who is in the grace of God, leads a supernatural life, more or less supernatural, according to his calling, and the measure of the gifts given him, and his faithfulness to them. This they know not, and admit not; and when they hear of the life which a Priest must lead by his profession from youth to age, they will not credit that he is what he professes to be. They know nothing of the presence of God, the merits of Christ, the intercession of the Blessed Virgin; the virtue of recurring prayers, of frequent confession, of daily Masses; they are strangers to the transforming power of the Most Holy Sacrament, the Bread of Angels; they do not contemplate the efficacy of salutary rules, of holy companions, of long-enduring habit, of ready spontaneous vigilance, of abhorrence of sin and indignation at the tempter, to secure the soul from evil. They only know that when the tempter once has actually penetrated into the heart, he is irresistible; they only know that when the soul has exposed and surrendered itself to his malice, there is (so to speak) a necessity of sinning. They only know that when God has abandoned it, and good Angels are withdrawn, and all safeguards, and protections, and preventives are neglected, that then (which is their own case), when the victory is all but gained already, it is sure to be gained altogether. They themselves have ever, in their best estate, been all but beaten by the Evil One before they began to fight; this is the only state they have experienced: they know this, and they know nothing else. They have never stood on vantage ground; they have never been within the walls of the strong city, about which the enemy prowls in vain, into which he cannot penetrate, and outside of which the faithful soul will be too wise to venture. They judge, I say, by their experience, and will not believe what they never knew.

If there be those here present, my dear brethren, who will not believe that grace is effectual within the Church, because it does little outside of it, to them I do not speak: I speak to those who do not narrow their belief to their experience; I speak to those who admit that grace can make human nature what it is not; and such persons, I think, will feel it, not a cause of jealousy and suspicion, but a great gain, a great mercy, that those are sent to preach to them, to receive their confessions, and to advise them, who can sympathise with their sins, even though they have not known them. Not a temptation, my brethren, can befall you, but what befalls all those who share your nature, though you may have yielded to it, and they may not have yielded. They can understand you, they can anticipate you, they can interpret you, though they have not kept pace with you in your course. They will be tender to you, they will "instruct you in the spirit of meekness," as the Apostle says, "considering themselves lest they also be tempted." Come then unto us, all ye that labour and are heavy laden, and ye shall find rest to your souls; come unto us, who now stand to you in Christ's stead, and who speak in Christ's name; for we too, like you, have been saved by Christ's all-saving blood. We too, like you, should be lost sinners, unless Christ had had mercy on us, unless His grace had cleansed us, unless His Church had received us, unless His saints had interceded for us. Be ye saved, as we have been saved; "come, listen, all ye that fear God, and we will tell you what He hath done for our souls." Listen to our testimony; behold our joy of heart, and increase it by partaking in it yourselves. Choose that good part which we have chosen; join ye yourselves to our company; it will never repent you, take our word for it, who have a right to speak, it will never repent you to have sought pardon and peace from the Catholic Church, which alone has grace, which alone has power, which alone has Saints; it will never repent you, though you go through trouble, though you have to give up much for her sake. It will never repent you, to have passed from the shadows of sense and time, and the deceptions of human feeling and false reason, to the glorious liberty of the sons of God.

And O, my brethren, when you have taken the great step, and stand in your blessed lot, as sinners reconciled to the Father you have offended (for I will anticipate, what I surely trust will be fulfilled as regards many of you), O then forget not those who have been the ministers of your reconciliation; and as they now pray you to make your peace with God, so do you, when reconciled, pray for them, that they may continue to stand in the grace in which they trust they stand now, even till the hour of death, lest, perchance, after they have preached to others, they themselves become reprobate.

Questions for Newman

1. Explain Newman's argument, at the beginning of his sermon, that since Christ was sinless, so also his representatives—his priests— must be as sinless as the holy angels. How does Newman then justify the fact that priests are not sinless?
2. Why does Newman consider penance and reconciliation to be the heart of the priesthood?
3. Why are repentant sinners, redeemed by God's grace, most suitable to minister to a flock that is in the same condition? What, according to Newman, can grace accomplish in human beings through God's ministers of reconciliation?

The Second Vatican Council

The Second Vatican Council met to renew the Catholic Church, and the Church is still experiencing the fruits of this renewal. "Lumen Gentium" is one of the two Dogmatic Constitutions produced by the Council, the other being "Dei Verbum" (on divine Revelation). Thus, "Lumen Gentium" offers an authoritative theology of the Church. The following excerpt, from chapter 3 ("On the Hierarchical Structure of the Church and in Particular on the Episcopate"), is especially helpful for understanding why the Church has an ordained priesthood, and how the bishops and the Pope (the bishop of Rome) are related.

18. For the nurturing and constant growth of the People of God, Christ the Lord instituted in his Church a variety of ministries, which work for the good of the whole body. For those ministers, who are endowed with a sacred power, serve their brethren, so that all who are of the People of God, and therefore enjoy a true Christian dignity, working toward a common goal freely and in an orderly way, may arrive at salvation.

This sacred Council, following closely in the footsteps of the First Vatican Council, with that Council teaches and declares that Jesus Christ, the eternal shepherd, established his holy Church, having sent forth the apostles as he himself had been sent by the Father (Jn 20:21), and he

From: "Lumen Gentium, The Dogmatic Constitution on the Church," in Marianne Lorraine Trouvé, FSP, ed., *The Sixteen Documents of Vatican II,* trans. N. C. W. C. (Boston: Pauline Books & Media, 1999), 143–156.

willed that their successors, namely the bishops, should be shepherds in his Church even to the consummation of the world. And in order that the episcopate itself might be one and undivided, he placed Blessed Peter over the other apostles, and instituted in him a permanent and visible source and foundation of unity of faith and communion.[1] And all this teaching about the institution, the perpetuity, the meaning and reason for the sacred primacy of the Roman Pontiff and of his infallible magisterium, this sacred Council again proposes to be firmly believed by all the faithful. Continuing in that same undertaking, this Council is resolved to declare and proclaim before all men the doctrine concerning bishops, the successors of the apostles, who together with the Successor of Peter, the Vicar of Christ,[2] the visible head of the whole Church, govern the house of the living God.

19. The Lord Jesus, after praying to the Father, calling to himself those whom he desired, appointed twelve to be with him, and whom he would send to preach the kingdom of God (Mk 3:13–19; Mt 10:1–42), and these apostles (cf. Lk 6:13) he formed after the manner of a college or a stable group, over which he placed Peter, chosen from among them (cf. Jn 21:15–17). He sent them first to the children of Israel and then to all nations (Rom 1:16), so that as sharers in his power they might make all peoples his disciples, and sanctify and govern them (cf. Mt 28:16–20; Mk 16:15; Lk 24:45–48; Jn 20:21–23), and thus spread his Church, and by ministering to it under the guidance of the Lord, direct it all days even to the consummation of the world (cf. Mt 28:20). And in this mission they were fully confirmed on the day of Pentecost (cf. Acts 2:1–26) in accordance with the Lord's promise: "You shall receive power when the Holy Spirit comes upon you, and you shall be witnesses for me in Jerusalem, and in all Judea and in Samaria, and even to the very ends of the earth" (Acts 1:8). And the apostles, by preaching the Gospel everywhere (cf. Mk 16:20), and it being accepted by their hearers under the influence of the Holy Spirit, gather together the universal Church, which the Lord established on the apostles and built upon Blessed Peter, their chief, Christ Jesus himself being the supreme cornerstone (cf. Rev 21:14; Mt 16:18; Eph 2:20).[3]

20. That divine mission, entrusted by Christ to the apostles, will last until the end of the world (cf. Mt 28:20), since the Gospel they are to teach is for all time the source of all life for the Church. And for this reason the apostles, appointed as rulers in this society, took care to appoint successors.

For they not only had helpers in their ministry[4] but also, in order that the mission assigned to them might continue after their death, they passed on to their immediate cooperators, as it were, in the form of a testament, the duty of confirming and finished the work begun by themselves,[5] recommending to them that they attend to the whole flock in which the Holy Spirit placed them to shepherd the Church of God (cf. Acts 20:28). They therefore appointed such men, and gave them the order that, when they should have died, other approved men would take up their ministry.[6] Among those various ministries which, according to tradition, were exercised in the Church from the earliest times, the chief place belongs to the office of those who, appointed to the episcopate, by a succession running from the beginning,[7] are passers-on of the apostolic seed.[8] Thus, as St. Irenaeus testifies, through those who were appointed bishops by the apostles, and through their successors down in our own time, the apostolic tradition is manifested[9] and preserved.[10]

Bishops, therefore, with their helpers, the priests and deacons, have taken up the service of the community,[11] presiding in place of God over the flock[12] whose shepherds they are, as teachers for doctrine, priests for sacred worship, and ministers for governing.[13] And just as the office granted individually to Peter, the first among the apostles, is permanent and is to be transmitted to his successors, so also the apostles' office of nurturing the Church is permanent, and is to be exercised without interruption by the sacred order of bishops.[14] Therefore, the sacred Council teaches that bishops by divine institution have succeeded to the place of the apostles,[15] as the shepherds of the Church, and he who hears them, hears Christ, and he who rejects them, rejects Christ and him who sent Christ (cf. Lk 10:16).[16]

21. In the bishops, therefore, for whom priests are assistants, our Lord Jesus Christ, the supreme high priest, is present in the midst of those who believe. For sitting at the right hand of God the Father, he is not absent from the gathering of his high priests,[17] but above all through their excellent service he is preaching the Word of God to all nations, and constantly administering the sacraments of faith to those who believe; by their paternal functioning (cf. 1 Cor. 4:15) he incorporates new members in his body by a heavenly regeneration, and finally by their wisdom and prudence he directs and guides the People of the New Testament in their pilgrimage toward eternal happiness. These pastors, chosen to shepherd the Lord's flock of the elect, are servants of

Christ and stewards of the mysteries of God (cf. 1 Cor 4:1), to whom has been assigned the bearing of witness to the Gospel of the grace of God (cf. Rom 15:16; Acts 20:24), and the ministration of the Spirit and of justice in glory (cf. 2 Cor 3:8–9).

For the discharging of such great duties, the apostles were enriched by Christ with a special outpouring of the Holy Spirit coming upon them (cf. Acts 1:8; 2:4; Jn 20:22–23), and they passed on this spiritual gift to their helpers by the imposition of hands (cf. 1 Tm 4:14; 2 Tm 1:6–7), and it has been transmitted down to us in episcopal consecration.[18] And the sacred Council teaches that by episcopal consecration the fullness of the sacrament of Orders is conferred, that fullness of power, namely, which both in the Church's liturgical practice and in the language of the Fathers of the Church is called the high priesthood, the supreme power of the sacred ministry.[19] But episcopal consecration, together with the office of sanctifying, also confers the office of teaching and governing, which, however, of its very nature, can be exercised only in hierarchical communion with the head and the members of the college. For from the tradition, which is expressed especially in liturgical rites and in the practice of both the Church of the East and of the West, it is clear that, by means of the imposition of hands and the words of consecration, the grace of the Holy Spirit is so conferred[20] and the sacred character so impressed[21] that bishops in an eminent and visible way sustain the roles of Christ himself as teacher, shepherd and high priest, and that they act in his person.[22] Therefore it pertains to the bishops to admit newly elected members into the episcopal body by means of the sacrament of Orders.

22. Just as in the Gospel, the Lord so disposing, St. Peter and the other apostles constitute one apostolic college, so in a similar way the Roman Pontiff, the Successor of Peter, and the bishops, the successors of the apostles, are joined together. Indeed, the very ancient practice whereby bishops duly established in all parts of the world were in communion with one another and with the Bishop of Rome in a bond of unity, charity and peace,[23] and also the councils assembled together,[24] in which more profound issues were settled in common,[25] the opinion of the many having been so prudently considered,[26] both of these factors are already an indication of the collegiate character and aspect of the episcopal order, and the ecumenical councils held in the course of centuries are also manifest proof of that same character. And it is intimated also

in the practice, introduced in ancient times, of summoning several bishops to take part in the elevation of the newly elected to the ministry of the high priesthood. Hence, one is constituted a member of the episcopal body in virtue of sacramental consecration and hierarchical communion with the head and members of the body.

But the college or body of bishops has no authority unless it is understood together with the Roman Pontiff, the Successor of Peter, as its head. The Pope's power of primacy over all, both pastors and faithful, remains whole and intact. In virtue of his office, that is as Vicar of Christ and pastor of the whole Church, the Roman Pontiff has full, supreme, and universal power over the Church. And he is always free to exercise this power. The order of bishops, which succeeds to the college of apostles and gives this apostolic body continued existence, is also the subject of supreme and full power over the universal Church, provided we understand this body together with its head the Roman Pontiff and never without this head.[27] This power can be exercised only with the consent of the Roman Pontiff. For our Lord placed Simon alone as the rock and the bearer of the keys of the Church (cf. Mt 16:18–19), and made him shepherd of the whole flock (cf. Jn 21:15 ff.); it is evident, however, that the power of binding and loosing, which was given to Peter (Mt 16:19), was granted also to the college of apostles, joined with their head (Mt 18:18; 28:16–20).[28] This college, insofar as it is composed of many, expresses the variety and universality of the People of God, but insofar as it is assembled under on head, it expresses the unity of the flock of Christ. In it, the bishops, faithfully recognizing the primacy and preeminence of their head, exercise their own authority for the good of their own faithful, and indeed of the whole Church, the Holy Spirit supporting its organic structure and harmony with moderation. The supreme power in the universal Church, which this college enjoys, is exercised in a solemn way in an ecumenical council. A council is never ecumenical unless it is confirmed or at least accepted as such by the Successor of Peter, and it is the prerogative of the Roman Pontiff to convoke these councils, to preside over them and to confirm them.[29] This same collegiate power can be exercised together with the Pope by the bishops living in all parts of the world, provided that the head of the college calls them to collegiate action, or at least approves of or freely accepts the united action of the scattered bishops, so that it is thereby made a collegiate act.

23. This collegial union is apparent also in the mutual relations of the individual bishops with particular churches and with the universal Church. The Roman Pontiff, as the Successor of Peter, is the perpetual and visible principle and foundation of unity of both the bishops and of the faithful.[30] The individual bishops, however, are the visible principle and foundation of unity in their particular churches,[31] fashioned after the model of the universal Church, in and from which churches come into being the one and only Catholic Church.[32] For this reason the individual bishops represent each his own church, but all of them together and with the Pope represent the entire Church in the bond of peace, love and unity.

The individual bishops, who are placed in charge of particular churches, exercise their pastoral government over the portion of the People of God committed to their care, and not over other churches nor over the universal Church. But each of them, as a member of the episcopal college and legitimate successor of the apostles, is obliged by Christ's institution and command to be solicitous for the whole Church,[33] and this solicitude, though it is not exercised by an act of jurisdiction, contributes greatly to the advantage of the universal Church. For it is the duty of all bishops to promote and to safeguard the unity of faith and the discipline common to the whole Church, to instruct the faithful to love for the whole Mystical Body of Christ, especially for its poor and sorrowing members and for those who are suffering persecution for justice's sake (cf. Mt 5:10), and finally to promote every activity that is of interest to the whole Church, especially that the faith may take increase and the light of full truth appear to all men. And this also is important, that by governing well their own church as a portion of the universal Church, they themselves are effectively contributing to the welfare of the whole Mystical Body, which is also the body of the churches.[34]

The task of proclaiming the Gospel everywhere on earth pertains to the body of pastors, to all of whom in common Christ gave his command, thereby imposing upon them a common duty, as Pope Celestine in his time recommended to the Fathers of the Council of Ephesus.[35] From this it follows that the individual bishops, insofar as their own discharge of their duty permits, are obliged to enter into a community of work among themselves and with the Successor of Peter, upon whom was imposed in a special way the great duty of spreading the Christian name.[36] With all their energy, therefore, they must supply to the missions both workers for the harvest and also spiritual and material aid, both directly and on their own account, as well as by arousing the ardent cooperation of the faithful. And finally, the bishops, in a universal fellowship of charity, should gladly extend their fraternal aid to other churches, especially to neighboring and more needy dioceses in accordance with the venerable example of antiquity.

By divine Providence it has come about that various churches, established in various places by the apostles and their successors, have in the course of time coalesced into several groups organically united, which preserving the unity of faith and the unique divine constitution of the universal Church, enjoy their own discipline, their own liturgical usage, and their own theological and spiritual heritage. Some of these churches, notably the ancient patriarchal churches, as parent-stocks of the faith, so to speak, have begotten others as daughter churches, with which they are connected down to our own time by a close bond of charity in their sacramental life and in their mutual respect for their rights and duties.[37] This variety of local churches with one common aspiration is splendid evidence of the catholicity of the undivided Church. In like manner the episcopal bodies of today are in a position to render a manifold and fruitful assistance, so that this collegiate feeling may be put into practical application.

24. Bishops, as successors of the apostles, receive from the Lord, to whom was given all power in heaven and on earth, the mission to teach all nations and to preach the Gospel to every creature, so that all men may attain to salvation by faith, Baptism and the fulfillment of the commandments (cf. Mt 28:18; Mk 16:15–16; Acts 26:17 ff.). To fulfill this mission, Christ the Lord promised the Holy Spirit to the apostles, and on Pentecost day sent the Spirit from heaven, by whose power they would be witnesses to him before the nations and peoples and kings even to the ends of the earth (cf. Acts 1:8; 2:1 ff.; 9:15). And that duty, which the Lord committed to the shepherds of his people, is a true service, which in sacred literature is significantly called "diakonia" or ministry (cf. Acts 1:17, 25; 21:19; Rom 11:13; 1 Tm 1:12).

The canonical mission of bishops can come about by legitimate customs that have not been revoked by the supreme and universal authority of the Church, or by laws made or recognized by that same authority, or directly through the Successor of Peter himself, and if the latter refuses or denies apostolic communion, such bishops cannot assume any office.[38]

25. Among the principal duties of bishops the preaching of the Gospel occupies an eminent place.[39] For bishops are preachers of the faith, who lead new disciples to Christ, and they are authentic teachers, that is, teachers endowed with the authority of Christ, who preach to the people committed to them the faith they must believe and put into practice, and by the light of the Holy Spirit illustrate that faith. They bring forth from the treasure of revelation new things and old (cf. Mt 13:52), making it bear fruit and vigilantly warding off any errors that threaten their flock (cf. 2 Tm 4:1–4). Bishops, teaching in communion with the Roman Pontiff, are to be respected by all as witnesses to divine and Catholic truth. In matters of faith and morals, the bishops speak in the name of Christ and the faithful are to accept their teaching and adhere to it with a religious assent. This religious submission of mind and will must be shown in a special way to the authentic magisterium of the Roman Pontiff, even when he is not speaking *ex cathedra*; that is, it must be shown in such a way that his supreme magisterium is acknowledged with reverence, the judgments made by him are sincerely adhered to, according to his manifest mind and will. His mind and will in the matter may be known either from the character of the documents, from his frequent repetition of the same doctrine, or from his manner of speaking.

Although the individual bishops do not enjoy the prerogative of infallibility, they nevertheless proclaim Christ's doctrine infallibly whenever, even though dispersed through the world, but still maintaining the bond of communion among themselves and with the Successor of Peter, and authentically teaching matters of faith and morals, they are in agreement on one position as definitively to be held.[40] This is even more clearly verified when, gathered together in an ecumenical council, they are teachers and judges of faith and morals for the universal Church, whose definitions must be adhered to with the submission of faith.[41]

And this infallibility with which the divine Redeemer willed his Church to be endowed in defining doctrine of faith and morals extends as far as the deposit of revelation extends, which must be religiously guarded and faithfully expounded. And this is the infallibility which the Roman Pontiff, the head of the college of bishops, enjoys in virtue of his office, when as the supreme shepherd and teacher of all the faithful, who confirms his brethren in their faith (cf. Lk 22:32), by a definitive act he proclaims a doctrine of faith or morals.[42] And therefore his definitions, of themselves, and not from the consent of the Church, are justly styled irreformable, since they are pronounced with the assistance of the Holy Spirit, promised to him in Blessed Peter, and therefore they need no approval of others, nor do they allow an appeal to any other judgment. For then the Roman Pontiff is not pronouncing judgment as a private person, but as the supreme teacher of the universal Church, in whom the charism of infallibility of the Church itself is individually present, he is expounding or defending a doctrine of Catholic faith.[43] The infallibility promised to the Church resides also in the body of bishops, when that body exercises the supreme magisterium with the Successor of Peter. To these definitions the assent of the Church can never be wanting, on account of the activity of that same Holy Spirit, by which the whole flock of Christ is preserved and progresses in unity of faith.[44]

But when either the Roman Pontiff or the body of bishops together with him defines a judgment, they pronounce it in accordance with revelation itself, which all are obliged to abide by and be in conformity with, that is, the revelation which as written or orally handed down is transmitted in its entirety through the legitimate succession of bishops and especially in care of the Roman Pontiff himself, and which under the guiding light of the Spirit of truth is religiously preserved and faithfully expounded in the Church.[45] The Roman Pontiff and the bishops, in view of their office and the importance of the matter, by fitting means diligently strive to inquire properly into that revelation and to give apt expression to its contents,[46] but a new public revelation they do not accept as pertaining to the divine deposit of faith.[47]

26. A bishop, marked with the fullness of the sacrament of Orders, is "the steward of the grace of the supreme priesthood,"[48] especially in the Eucharist, which he offers or causes to be offered[49] and by which the Church continually lives and grows. This Church of Christ is truly present in all legitimate local congregations of the faithful which, united with their pastors, are themselves called churches in the New Testament.[50] For in their locality these are the new people called by God, in the Holy Spirit and in much fullness (cf. 1 Thes. 1:5). In them the faithful are gathered together by the preaching of the Gospel of Christ, and the mystery of the Lord's Supper is celebrated, that by the food and Blood of the Lord's Body the whole brotherhood may be joined together.[51] In any community of the altar, under the sacred ministry of the bishop,[52] there is exhibited a symbol of that charity and "unity of the Mystical Body, without which there can be no salvation."[53] In these

communities, though frequently small and poor, or living in the Diaspora, Christ is present, and in virtue of his presence there is brought together one, holy, catholic and apostolic Church.[54] For "the partaking of the Body and Blood of Christ does nothing other than make us be transformed into that which we consume."[55]

Every legitimate celebration of the Eucharist is regulated by the bishop, to whom is committed the office of offering the worship of Christian religion to the divine majesty and of administering it in accordance with the Lord's commandments and the Church's laws, as further defined by his particular judgment for his diocese.

Bishops, thus, by praying and laboring for the people, make outpourings in many ways and in great abundance from the fullness of Christ's holiness. By the ministry of the Word they communicate God's power to those who believe unto salvation (cf. Rom 1:16), and through the sacraments, the regular and fruitful distribution of which they regulate by their authority,[56] they sanctify the faithful. They direct the conferring of Baptism, by which a sharing in the kingly priesthood of Christ is granted. They are the original ministers of Confirmation, dispensers of sacred Orders and the moderators of penitential discipline, and they earnestly exhort and instruct their people to carry out with faith and reverence their part in the liturgy and especially in the holy sacrifice of the Mass. And lastly, by the example of their way of life they must be an influence for good to those over whom they preside, refraining from all evil, and as far as they are able with God's help, exchanging evil for good, so that together with the flock committed to their care they may arrive at eternal life.[57]

27. Bishops, as vicars and ambassadors of Christ, govern the particular churches entrusted to them[58] by their counsel, exhortations, example and even by their authority and sacred power, which indeed they use only for the edification of their flock in truth and holiness, remembering that he who is greater should become as the lesser and he who is the chief become as the servant (cf. Lk 22:26–27). This power, which they personally exercise in Christ's name, is proper, ordinary and immediate, although its exercise is ultimately regulated by the supreme authority of the Church, and can be circumscribed by certain limits, for the advantage of the Church or of the faithful. In virtue of this power, bishops have the sacred right and the duty before the Lord to make laws for their subjects, to pass judgment on them and to moderate everything pertaining to the ordering of worship and the apostolate.

The pastoral office or the habitual and daily care of their sheep is entrusted to them completely; nor are they to be regarded as vicars of the Roman Pontiffs, for they exercise an authority that is proper to them, and are quite correctly called "prelates," heads of the people whom they govern.[59] Their power, therefore, is not destroyed by the supreme and universal power, but on the contrary, it is affirmed, strengthened and vindicated by it[60] since the Holy Spirit unfailingly preserves the form of government established by Christ the Lord in his Church.

A bishop, since he is sent by the Father to govern his family, must keep before his eyes the example of the good shepherd, who came not to be ministered unto but to minister (cf. Mt 20:28; Mk 10:45), and to lay down his life for his sheep (cf. Jn 10:11). Being taken from among men, and himself beset with weakness, he is able to have compassion on the ignorant and erring (cf. Heb 5:1–2). Let him not refuse to listen to his subjects, whom he cherishes as his true sons and exhorts to cooperate readily with him. As having one day to render an account for their souls (cf. Heb 13:17), he takes care of them by his prayer, preaching and all the works of charity, and not only of them but also of those who are not yet of the one flock, who also are commended to him in the Lord. Since, like Paul the Apostle, he is debtor to all men, let him be ready to preach the Gospel to all (cf. Rom 1:14–15), and to urge his faithful to apostolic and missionary activity. But the faithful must cling to their bishop, as the Church does to Christ, and Jesus Christ to the Father, so that all may be of one mind through unity[61] and abound to the glory of God (cf. 2 Cor 4:15).

Questions for the Second Vatican Council

1. What does the Council teach about Christ's institution of the Church? How did Christ structure the Church? Why did he do so?
2. How is Christ present in his Church through the bishops? According to the Council, what are the proper tasks of the bishops? How should a bishop relate to his flock, and vice versa?
3. Describe the relationship of the Pope, successor of Peter, and the body of bishops. What is the "magisterium" and what authority does it possess for believers? Describe the role of "infallibility" in the Church, according to the Council.

Notes

1. Cf. First Vatican Ecumenical Council, session 4, Constitution *Pastor Aeternus*, Denz. 1821 (3050 f.).

2. Cf. Council of Florence, *Decretum pro Graecis*, Denz. 694 (1307) and First Vatican Ecumenical Council, ibid.: Denz. 1826 (3059).

3. Cf. *Liber Sacramentorum*, St. Gregory, *Praefatio in Cathedra St. Petri*, in *Natali St. Mathiae et St. Thomas*: PL 78, 50, 51 and 152; cf. Cod. Vat. Lat. 3548, f. 18; St. Hilary, *In Ps.* 67, 10: PL 9, 450; CSEL 22, 286; St. Jerome, *Adv. Iovin.* 1, 26: PL 23, 247 A; St. Augustine, *In Ps.* 86, 4: PL 37, 1103; St. Gregory the Great, *Mor. In Job*, XXVIII, V: PL 76, 455-456; Primasius, *Comm. In Apoc.*, V: PL 68, 924 B, C; Paschasius Radbertus, *In Matth.* Bk. VIII, ch. 16: PL 120, 561 C; cf. Leo XIII, Epistle *Et Sane* (Dec. 17, 1888): AAS 21 (1888), 321.

4. Cf. Acts 6:2-6; 11:30; 13:1; 14:23; 20:17; 1 Thes 5:12-13; Phil 1:1; Col 4:11 and *passim*.

5. Cf. Acts 20:25-27; 2 Tm 4:6 f. together with 1 Tm 5:22; 2 Tm 2:2; Ti 1:5; St. Clement of Rome, *Ad Cor.* 44, 3; ed. F. X. Funk, I, 156.

6. St. Clement of Rome, *Ad Cor.* 44, 2; ed. F. X. Funk, I, 154 f.

7. Cf. Tertullian, *Praescr. Haer.* 32: PL 2, 52 f.; St. Ignatius Martyr, *passim*.

8. Cf. Tertullian, *Praescr. Haer.* 32: PL 2, 53.

9. Cf. St. Irenaeus, *Against Heretics* III, 3, 1: PG 7, 848 A, Harvey 2, 8, ed. Sagnard, 100 f., "*manifestatam*."

10. Cf. St. Irenaeus, *Against Heretics* III, 2, 2: PG 7, 847, Harvey 2, 7, ed. Sagnard, 100, "*custoditur*"; cf. *ibid.* IV, 26, 2; col. 1053, Harvey 2, 236 and IV, 33, 8; col. 1077; Harvey 2, 262.

11. St. Ignatius Martyr, *Philad.* Praef.; ed. F. X. Funk, I, 264.

12. St. Ignatius Martyr, *Philad.* 1, 1; *Magn.* 6, 1; ed. F. X. Funk, I, 264 and 234.

13. St. Clement of Rome, 1. c., 42, 3-4; 44, 3-4; 57, 1-2; ed. F. X. Funk, I, 152, 156, 171 f.; St. Ignatius Martyr, *Philad.* 2; *Smyrn.* 8; *Magn.* 3; *Trall.* 7; ed. F. X. Funk, I 265 f., 282; 232, 246 f. etc.; St. Justin, *Apol.* 1, 65; PG 6, 428; St. Cyprian, *Epist., passim*.

14. Cf. Leo XIII, Encyclical Epistle *Satis Cognitum* (Jan. 29, 1896): AAS 28 (1895–1896), 732.

15. Cf. Council of Trent, Session 23, Decree *De Sacr. Ordinis*, ca. 4; Denz. 960 (1768); First Vatican Ecumenical Council, Session 4, Dogmatic Constitution *De Ecclesia Christi*, ca. 3: Denz. 1828 (3061); Pius XII, Encyclical Letter *Mystici Corporis* (June 29, 1943): AAS 35 (1943), 209 and 212; *Code of Canon Law*, c. 329 & 1.

16. Cf. Leo XIII, Epistle *Et Sane* (Dec. 17, 1888): AAS 21 (1888), 321 f.

17. St. Leo the Great, *Serm.* 5, 3: PL 54, 154.

18. Council of Trent, Session 23, c. 3, cites the words of 2 Tm 1:6–7, to show that Orders is a true sacrament: Denz. 959 (1766).

19. In the *Apostolic Tradition*, 3, ed. Botte, *Sources Chr.*, 27–30, "to the bishop is attributed 'primacy of priesthood.'" Cf. *Sacramentarium Leonianum*, ed. L. C. Mohlberg, *Sacramentarium Veronens* (Rome: 1955), 119: "To the ministry of high priesthood . . . Fulfill in your priests the fullness of the mystery." *Idem. Liber Sacramentorum Romanae Ecclesiae* (Rome: 1960), 121–122: "Grant them, Lord, the bishop's throne to rule your Church and all people." Cf. PL 78, 224.

20. *Apostolic Tradition*, 2, ed. Botte, 27.

21. Council of Trent, Session 23, c. 4, teaches that the sacrament of Orders imprints an indelible character: Denz. 960 (1767). Cf. John XXIII, *Allocution Jubilate Deo* (May 8, 1960): *AAS* 52 (1960), 466; Paul VI, *Homily* in St. Peter's Bascilica (Oct. 20, 1963): *AAS* 55 (1963), 1014.

22. St. Cyprian, *Epist.* 63, 14: PL 4, 386; Hartel, III B, 713: "The priest truly acts in the place of Christ"; St. John Chrysostom, *In 2 Tm*, Hom. 2, 4: PG 62, 612: "The priest is a 'symbolon' of Christ." St. Ambrose, *In Ps.* 38, 25–26: PL 14, 105, 1–52; CSEL 64, 203-204; Ambrosiaster, *In 1 Tm* 5, 19: PL 17, 479 C and *In Eph.* 4:11–12: col. 387 C; Theodore of Mopsuestia, *Hom. Catech.* XV, 21 and 24: ed. Tonneau, 497 and 503; Hesychius of Jerusalem, *In Lev.* L. 2, 9, 23: PG 93, 894 B.

23. Cf. Eusebius, *Hist. Eccl.*, V, 24, 10: GCS II, 1, 495; ed. Bardy, *Sources Chr.* II, 69; Dionysius, as given in Eusebius, ibid. VII 5, 2: GCS 11, 2, 638 f.; Bardy, II, 168 f.

24. For the ancient councils, cf. Eusebius, *Hist. Eccl.*, V, 23-24: GCS 11, 1, 488 ff.; Bardy, 11, 66 ff. and *passim*. Council of Nicea, can. 5: *Conc. Oec. Decr.* 7.

25. Tertullian, *De Ieiunio* 13: PL 2, 972 B; CSEL 20, 292, lin. 13–16.

26. St. Cyprian, *Epist.* 56, 3: Hartel, III B, 650; Bayard, 154.

27. Cf. Zinelli, *Relatio officialis*, on First Vatican Ecumenical Council: Mansi 52, 1109 C.

28. Cf. First Vatican Ecumenical Council, *Schema* on the Dogmatic Constitution II, *De Ecclesia Ch*risti, c. 4: Mansi 53, 310. Cf. Kleutgen's account of the reformed schema: Mansi 53, 321 B–322 B and Zinelli's *Declaratio*: Mansi 52, 1110 A. Cf. also St. Leo the Great, *Serm.* 4, 3: PL 54, 151 A.

29. Cf. *Code of Canon Law*, c. 227.

30. Cf. First Vatican Ecumenical Council, Constitution *Pastor Aeternus*: Denz. 1821 (3050 f.).

31. Cf. St. Cyprian, *Epist.* 6, 8: Hartel III, 2, 733: "The bishop is in the Church and the Church in the bishop."

32. Cf. St. Cyprian, *Epist.* 55, 24: Hartel, 642, lin. 13: "One Church throughout the whole world divided into many members." *Epist.* 36, 4: Hartel, 575, lin. 20–21.

33. Cf. Pius XII, Encyclical Letter *Fidei Donum* (April 21, 1957): AAS 49 (1957), 237.

34. Cf. St. Hilary of Poitiers, *In Ps.* 14, 3: PL 9, 206; CSEL 22, 86; St. Gregory the Great, *Moral.*, IV, 7, 12: PL 75, 643 C; Pseudo Basil, *In Is.* 15, 296: PG 30, 637 C.

35. St. Celestine, *Epist.* 18, 1-2, to the Council of Ephesus: PL 50, 505 AB, Schwartz, *Acta Conc. Oec.* I, 1, 1, 22; cf. Benedict XV, Apostolic Letter *Maximum Illud*: AAS 11 (1919), 440; Pius XI, Encyclical Letter *Rerum Ecclesiae* (Feb. 28, 1926): AAS 18 (1926), 69; Pius XII, Encyclical Letter *Fidei Donum* (April 21, 1957): AAS 49 (1957), 237.

36. Leo XIII, Encyclical Letter *Grande Munus* (Sept. 30, 1880): AAS 13 (1880), 145; cf. *Code of Canon Law*, c. 1327; c. 1350 par. 2.

37. On the rights of patriarchal Sees, cf. Council of Nicea, can. 6 on Alexandria and Antioch, and can. 7 on Jerusalem: *Conc. Oec. Decr.*, 8; Fourth Lateran Council (1215), Constit. V: *De Dignitate Patriarcharum:* ibid., 212; Council of Ferrara-Florence: ibid., 504.

38. Cf. *Code of Canon Law for the Eastern Churches*, c. 216–314: regarding patriarchs; c. 324–399: on major archbishops; c. 362–391: regarding other dignitaries, in particular, c. 238 13; 216; 240; 251; 255: regarding bishops to be named by patriarchs.

39. Cf. Council of Trent, Session 5, *Decr. De Reform.*, c. 2, n. 9; and Session 24, can. 4; *Conc. Oec. Decr.*, 645 and 739.

40. Cf. First Vatican Ecumenical Council, Session III, Constitution *Dei Filius*, Denz. 1712 (3011). Cf. the note added to Schema I *De Ecclesia* (taken from St. Robert Bellarmine): Mansi 51, I 579; cf. also the revised Schema of Const. II *De Ecclesia Christi*, with the commentary by Kleutgen: Mansi 53, 313 AB; Pius IX, Letter *Tuas Libenter:* Denz. 1683 (2879).

41. Cf. *Code of Canon Law*, c. 1322–1323.

42. Cf. First Vatican Ecumenical Council, Constitution *Pastor Aeternus*: Denz. 1839 (3074).

43. Cf. the explanation by Gasser of First Vatican Ecumenical Council: Mansi 52, 1213 AC.

44. Gasser, ibid.: Mansi 1214 A.

45. Gasser, ibid.: Mansi 1215 CD, 1216–1217 A.

46. Gasser, ibid.: Mansi 1213.

47. First Vatican Ecumenical Council, Constitution *Pastor Aeternus*: Denz. 1836 (3070) no. 26.

48. Prayer of episcopal consecration in the Byzantine rite: *Euchologion to mega*, Rome, 1873, 139.

49. Cf. St. Ignatius Martyr, *Smyrn.* 8, 1: ed. F. X. Funk, I, 282.

50. Cf. Acts 8:1; 14:22–23; 20:17, and *passim.*

51. Mozarabic prayer: PL 96, 759 B.

52. Cf. St. Ignatius Martyr, *Smyrn.* 8, 1: ed. F. X. Funk, I, 282.

53. St. Thomas, *Summa Theol.*, III, q. 73, a. 3.

54. Cf. St. Augustine, *C. Faustum* 12, 20: PL 42, 265; *Serm.* 57, 7: PL 38, 389, etc.

55. St. Leo the Great, *Serm.* 63, 7: PL 54, 357 C.

56. *Apostolic Tradition* of Hippolytus, 2–3: ed. Botte, 26–30.

57. Cf. the text of the *examen* at the beginning of the consecration of a bishop, and the prayer at the end of the Mass of the same consecration, after the *Te Deum.*

58. Benedict XIV, Brief *Romana Ecclesia* (Oct. 5, 1752), 1: *Bullarium Benedicti XIV*, t. IV, Rome, 1758, 21: "The bishop represents Christ, and acts by his authority"; Pius XII, Encyclical Letter *Mystici Corporis* (June 29, 1943): *AAS* 35 (1943), 211: "Each of them, in the name of Christ, feeds and rules the particular flock assigned to him."

59. Leo XIII, Encyclical Epistle *Satis Cognitum* (Jan. 29, 1896): *AAS* 28 (1895–96), 732; Leo XIII, Letter *Officio Sanctissimo* (Dec. 22, 1887): *AAS* 20 (1887), 264; Pius IX, Apostolic Letter to the bishops of Germany (March 12, 1875) and his Consistorial Allocution (March 15, 1875): Denz. 3112–3117, only in the new edition.

60. First Vatican Ecumenical Council, Constitution *Pastor Aeternus*, 3: Denz. 1828 (3061); cf. Zinelli, *Relatio*, Mansi 52, 1114 D.

61. Cf. St. Ignatius Martyr, *Ad Ephes.* 5, 1: ed. F. X. Funk, I, 216.

Pope John Paul II

One of the great spiritual leaders of the twentieth century, Pope John
Paul II (Karol Wojtyla) was ordained a priest in 1946, and became
Pope in 1978. The author of poetry, plays, and philosophical works,
as well as a wide variety of writings during his papacy, John Paul II
provides unique insight into the mystery of the priesthood as lived
out in the second half of the twentieth century. His vision is richly
Christological and focuses upon the need for holiness, in light of the
gifts of the Holy Spirit.

Who Is the Priest?

IN THIS PERSONAL TESTIMONY, I feel the need to go beyond the mere rec-
ollection of events and individuals in order to take a deeper look and
to search out, as it were, the mystery which for fifty years has accompanied and enfolded me.

What does it mean to be a priest? According to Saint Paul, it means
above all to be a *steward of the mysteries of God*: "This is how one should
regard us, as servants of Christ and stewards of the mysteries of God.
Now it is required of stewards that they be found trustworthy" (1 Cor.

4:1–2). The word "steward" cannot be replaced by any other. It is deeply rooted in the Gospel: it brings to mind the parable of the faithful steward and the unfaithful one (cf. Lk 12:41–48). The steward is not the owner, but the one to whom the owner entrusts his goods so that he will manage them justly and responsibly. In exactly the same way, the priest receives from Christ the treasures of salvation, in order duly to distribute them among the people to whom he is sent. These treasures are those of faith. The priest is thus a man of the word of God, a man of sacrament, a man of the "mystery of faith." Through faith he draws near to the invisible treasures which constitute the inheritance of the world's Redemption by the Son of God. No one may consider himself the "owner" of these treasures; they are meant for us all. But, by reason of what Christ laid down, the priest has the task of administering them.

Admirabile Commercium!

The priestly vocation is a mystery. It is the mystery of a "wondrous exchange"—*admirabile commercium*—between God and man. A man offers his humanity to Christ, so that Christ may use him as an instrument of salvation, making him as it were into another Christ. Unless we grasp the mystery of this "exchange," we will not understand how it can be that a young man, hearing the words "Follow me!," can give up everything for Christ, in the certainty that if he follows this path he will find complete personal fulfillment.

In our world, is there any greater fulfillment of our humanity than to be able to re-present every day *in persona Christi* the redemptive sacrifice, the same sacrifice which Christ offered on the Cross? In this sacrifice, on the one hand, the very mystery of the Trinity is present in the most profound way, and, on the other hand, the entire created universe is "united" (cf. Eph. 1:10). The Eucharist is also celebrated in order to offer "on the altar of the whole earth the world's work and suffering," in the beautiful expression of Teilhard de Chardin. This is why in the thanksgiving after Holy Mass the Old Testament canticle of the three young men is recited: *Benedicite omnia opera Domini Domino*. For in the Eucharist all creatures seen and unseen, and man in particular, bless God as Creator and Father; they bless him with the words and the action of Christ, the Son of God.

The Priest and the Eucharist

"I thank you, Father, Lord of heaven and earth, that you have hidden these things from the wise and understanding and revealed them to babes. . . . No one knows who the Son is except the Father, or who the Father is except the Son and any one to whom the Son chooses to reveal him" (Lk 10:21–22). These words of Saint Luke's Gospel lead us to the heart of the mystery of Christ and enable us to draw near to the mystery of the Eucharist. In the Eucharist, the Son, who is of one being with the Father, the One whom only the Father knows, offers himself in sacrifice to the Father for humanity and for all creation. In the Eucharist Christ gives back to the Father everything that has come from him. Thus there is brought about a profound *mystery of justice on the part of the creature towards the Creator*. Man needs to honor his Creator by offering to him, in an act of thanksgiving and praise, all that he has received. *Man must never lose sight of his debt*, which he alone, among all other earthly realities, is capable of acknowledging and paying back as the one creature made in God's own image and likeness. At the same time, given his creaturely limitations and sinful condition, man would be incapable of making this act of justice towards the Creator, had not Christ himself, the Son who is of one being with the Father and also true man, first given us the Eucharist.

The priesthood, in its deepest reality, *is the priesthood of Christ*. It is Christ who offers himself, his Body and Blood, in sacrifice to God the Father, and by this sacrifice makes righteous in the Father's eyes all mankind and, indirectly, all creation. The priest, in his daily celebration of the Eucharist, goes to the very heart of this mystery. For this reason the celebration of the Eucharist must be the most important moment of the priest's day, the center of his life.

In Persona Christi

The words which we repeat at the end of the Preface—"Blessed is he who comes in the name of the Lord"—take us back to the dramatic events of Palm Sunday. Christ goes to Jerusalem to face the bloody sacrifice of Good Friday. But the day before, at the Last Supper, he institutes the sacrament of this sacrifice. Over the bread and wine he says the words of consecration: "This is my Body, which will be given up for you. . . . This is the cup of my Blood, the Blood of the new and everlasting covenant. It will be shed for you and for all so that sins may be forgiven. Do this in memory of me."

What kind of a "memorial" is this? We know that this term must be given a weighty significance, one which goes far beyond mere historical remembrance. Here we are speaking of a "memorial" in the biblical sense, a memorial which *makes present* the event itself. It is *memory* and *presence*. The secret of this miracle is the action of the Holy Spirit, whom the priest invokes when he extends his hands over the gifts of bread and wine: "Let *your Spirit* come upon these gifts to make them holy, so that they may become for us the Body and Blood of our Lord Jesus Christ." Thus it is not merely the priest who recalls the events of Christ's Passion, Death, and Resurrection; it is also the Holy Spirit who enables this event to be made present on the altar through the ministry of the priest. The priest truly *acts in persona Christi*. What Christ accomplished on the altar of the Cross and what earlier still he had instituted as a sacrament in the Upper Room, the priest now renews by the power of the Holy Spirit. At this moment the priest is as it were embraced by the power of the Holy Spirit, and the words which he utters have the same efficacy as those spoken by Christ at the Last Supper.

Mysterium Fidei

At Holy Mass, after the consecration, the priest says the words *Mysterium fidei, Let us proclaim the mystery of faith*! These words refer of course to the Eucharist. In a way, however, they also concern the priesthood. There can be no Eucharist without the priesthood, just as there can be no priesthood without the Eucharist. Not only is the ministerial priesthood closely linked to the Eucharist, but the common priesthood of all the baptized is also rooted in this mystery. To the celebrant's words the people reply: "When we eat this bread and drink this cup we proclaim your death, Lord Jesus, until you come in glory." As the Second Vatican Council reminded us, the faithful, by their sharing in the Eucharistic Sacrifice, become witnesses of the Crucified and Risen Christ and commit themselves to living his threefold mission—as priest, prophet, and king—which they received at Baptism.

The priest, as steward of the "mysteries of God," is at the service of the common priesthood of the faithful. By proclaiming the word and celebrating the sacraments, especially the Eucharist, he makes the whole People of God ever more aware of its share in Christ's priesthood, and at the same time encourages it to live that priesthood to the full. When, after the consecration, he says the words *Mysterium fidei*, all are invited to ponder the rich existential meaning of this proclamation, which refers to the mystery of Christ, the Eucharist, and the priesthood.

Is this not the deepest reason behind the priestly vocation? Certainly it is already fully present at the time of ordination, but it needs to be interiorized and deepened for the rest of the priest's life. Only in this way can a priest discover in depth the great treasure which has been entrusted to him. Fifty years after my ordination, I can say that in the words *Mysterium fidei* we find ever more each day the meaning of our own priesthood, and here is also the measure of the response which this gift demands. *The gift is constantly growing!* And this is something wonderful. It is wonderful that a man can never say that he has fully responded to the gift. It remains both a gift and a task: always! To be conscious of this is essential if we are to live our own priesthood to the full.

Christ, Priest and Victim

The truth about Christ's priesthood has always struck me in an extraordinarily eloquent way in the Litany which used to be recited in the seminary at Cracow, especially on the eve of a priestly ordination. I am referring to the *Litany of Our Lord Jesus Christ, Priest and Victim*. What profound reflections it prompted! In the Sacrifice of the Cross, made present anew in every Eucharist, Christ offers himself for the salvation of the world. The invocations of the Litany call to mind the many aspects of this mystery. They come back to me with all the rich symbolism of the biblical images with which they are interwoven. When I repeat them, it is in Latin, the language in which I recited them at the seminary and then so often in later years:

Iesu, Sacerdos et Victima,
Iesu, Sacerdos in aeternum secundum ordinem Melchisedech,
Iesu, Pontifex ex hominibus assumpte,
Iesu, Pontifex pro hominibus constitute,
Iesu, Pontifex futurorum bonorum,

Iesu, Pontifex fidelis et misericors,
Iesu, Pontifex qui dilexisti nos et lavisti nos a peccatis in sanguine tuo,
Iesu, Pontifex qui tradidisti temetipsum Deo oblationem et hostiam,
Iesu, Hostia sancta et immaculata,
Iesu, Hostia in qua habemus fiduciam et accessum ad Deum,
Iesu, Hostia vivens in saecula saeculorum.

What theological depth is present in these expressions! They are *invocations deeply rooted in Sacred Scripture*, especially in the Letter to the Hebrews. We need only reread this passage: "Christ . . . as a high priest of the good things to come . . . entered once for all into the Holy Place, taking not the blood of goats and calves but his own blood, thus securing an eternal redemption. For if the sprinkling of defiled persons with the blood of goats and bulls . . . sanctifies for the purification of the flesh, how much more shall the blood of Christ, who through the eternal Spirit offered himself without blemish to God, purify our conscience from dead works to serve the living God" (Heb 9:11–14). *Christ is a priest because he is the Redeemer of the world.* The priesthood of all presbyters is part of the mystery of the Redemption. This truth about Redemption and the Redeemer has been central to me; it has been with me all these years; it has permeated all my pastoral experiences, and it has continued to reveal new riches to me.

In these fifty years of priestly life, I have come to realize that the Redemption, the price which had to be paid for sin, entails *a renewed discovery, a kind of a "new creation" of the whole created order*: the rediscovery of man as a person, of man created by God as male and female, a rediscovery of the deepest truth about all man's works, his culture and civilization, about all his achievements and creative abilities.

After I was elected Pope, my first spiritual impulse was to turn to Christ the Redeemer. This was the origin of the Encyclical Letter *Redemptor Hominis*. As I reflect on all these events, I see ever more clearly the close link between the message of that Encyclical and everything that is found in the heart of man through his sharing in Christ's priesthood.

Being a Priest Today

Fifty years as a priest is a long time. How much has happened in this half-century of history! New problems, new lifestyles, and new challenges have appeared. And so it is natural to ask: What does it mean to be a priest *today*, in this time of constant change, as we approach the Third Millennium?

Certainly the priest, together with the whole Church, is part of the times in which he lives; he needs to be attentive and sympathetic, but also critical and watchful, with regard to historical developments. The Council has pointed to the possibility and need for an authentic renewal, in complete fidelity to the word of God and Tradition. But I am convinced that a priest, committed as he is to this necessary pastoral renewal, should at the same time have no fear of being "behind the times," because the human "today" of every priest is included in the "today" of Christ the Redeemer. For every priest, in every age, the greatest task is each day to discover his own priestly "today" in the "today" of Christ to which the Letter to the Hebrews refers. This "today" of Christ is immersed in the whole of history—in the past and future of the world, of every human being and of every priest. "Jesus Christ is the same yesterday and today and forever" (Heb 13:8). If we immerse our human and priestly "today" in the "today" of Jesus Christ, there is no danger that we will become out-of-date, belonging to "yesterday." Christ is the measure of every age. In his divine, human, and priestly "today," the conflict between "traditionalism" and "progressivism"—once so hotly debated—finds its ultimate resolution.

Humanity's Profound Expectations

If we take a close look at what contemporary men and women expect from priests, we will see that, in the end, they have but one great expectation: *they are thirsting for Christ.* Everything else—their economic, social, and political needs—can be met by any number of other people. From the priest they ask for Christ! And from him they have the right to receive Christ, above all through the proclamation of the word. As the Council teaches, priests "have as their primary duty the proclamation of the Gospel of God to all" (*Presbyterorum Ordinis*, 4). But this proclamation seeks to have man encounter Jesus, especially in the mystery of the Eucharist, the living heart of the Church and of priestly life. The priest has a mysterious, awesome power over the Eucharistic Body of Christ. By reason of this power he becomes the steward of the greatest treasure of the Redemption, for he gives people the Redeemer in person. Celebrating the Eucharist is the most sublime and most sacred function of every priest. As for me, from the very first years of my priesthood, the celebration of the Eucharist has been not only my most sacred duty, but above all my soul's deepest need.

A Minister of Mercy

As the steward of the *Sacrament of Reconciliation*, the priest fulfills the command given by Christ to the Apostles after his Resurrection: "Receive the Holy Spirit. If you forgive the sins of any, they are forgiven; if you retain the sins of any, they are retained" (Jn 20:22–23). The priest is the witness and instrument of divine mercy! How important in his life is the ministry of the confessional! It is in the confessional that *his spiritual fatherhood* is realized in the fullest way. It is in the confessional that every priest becomes a witness of the great miracles which divine mercy works in souls which receive the grace of conversion. It is necessary, however, that every priest at the service of his brothers and sisters in the confessional should experience this same divine mercy by going regularly to confession himself and by receiving spiritual direction.

As a steward of God's mysteries, the priest is a special *witness to the Invisible* in the world. For he is a steward of invisible and priceless treasures belonging to the spiritual and supernatural order.

A Man in Contact with God

As a steward of these treasures, the priest is always in special contact with *the holiness of God*. "Holy, holy, holy Lord, God of power and might, heaven and earth are full of your glory." God's majesty is the majesty of holiness. In the priesthood a man is as it were raised up to the sphere of this holiness; in some way he reaches the heights to which the Prophet Isaiah was once exalted. And it is precisely this vision of the Prophet which is echoed in the Eucharistic Liturgy: *Sanctus, Sanctus, Sanctus, Dominus Deus Sabaoth. Pleni sunt caeli et terra gloria tua. Hosanna in excelsis.*

At the same time, the priest experiences daily and continually the descent of God's holiness upon man: *Benedictus qui venit in nomine Domini*. With these words the crowds in Jerusalem greeted Christ as he came into the city to accomplish the sacrifice which brought Redemption to the world. Transcendent holiness, which is in a sense "outside the world," becomes in Christ a holiness which is "in the world." It becomes the holiness of the Paschal Mystery.

Called to Holiness

Constantly in contact with the holiness of God, the priest must himself become holy. His very ministry commits him to a way of life inspired by the radicalism of the Gospel. This explains his particular need to live in the spirit of the evangelical counsels of chastity, poverty, and obedience. Here we also see the special fittingness of celibacy. We also see the particular need for prayer in his life: prayer finds its source in God's holiness and is at the same time our response to this holiness. I once wrote "Prayer makes the priest and through prayer the priest becomes himself." Before all else the priest must indeed be a *man of prayer*, convinced that time devoted to personal encounter with God is always spent in the best way possible. This not only benefits him; it also benefits his apostolic work.

While the Second Vatican Council speaks of the *universal* call to holiness, in the case of the priest we must speak of a *special* call to holiness. *Christ needs holy priests*! Today's world demands holy priests! Only a holy priest can become, in an increasingly secularized world, a resounding witness to Christ and his Gospel. And only thus can a priest become a guide for men and women and a teacher of holiness. People, especially the young, are looking for such guides. A priest can be a guide and teacher only to the extent that he becomes an authentic witness!

Cura Animarum

My now long experience, amid so many different situations, has confirmed my conviction that *priestly holiness alone is the soil which can nourish an effective pastoral activity, a true "cura animarum."* The truest secret of authentic pastoral success does not lie in material means, much less in sophisticated programs. The lasting results of pastoral endeavors are born of the holiness of the priest. This is the foundation! Needless to say, training, study, and updating are indispensable; in short, an adequate preparation which enables one to respond to urgent needs and to discern *pastoral priorities*. But it can also be said that priorities depend on circumstances, and every priest is called to identify and pursue them under the authority of his Bishop and in harmony with the directives of the universal Church. In my own life I have identified these priorities in the lay apostolate and particularly in the pastoral care of the family—an area in which lay people themselves have helped me so much—in youth ministry and in serious dialogue with the world of learning and culture. All this has been reflected in my scholarly and literary activity. This was the origin of my study *Love and Responsibility* and, among others, the literary work *The Jeweler's Shop*, which is subtitled *Meditations on the Sacrament of Marriage*.

An inescapable priority today is that of preferential concern for the poor, the marginalized, and immigrants. The priest must be truly a "father" to such people. Material means are of course indispensable, such as those offered by modern technology. But the real secret is always the priest's holiness of life, which finds expression in prayer and meditation, in a spirit of sacrifice and in missionary zeal. When I think back on my years of pastoral ministry as priest and Bishop, I become more and more convinced of how true and fundamental this is.

A Man of the Word

I have already mentioned that, to be an authentic guide of the community and a true steward of the mysteries of God, the priest is also called to be a *man of God's word*, a generous and tireless evangelizer. Today the urgency of this is seen even more clearly in the light of the immense task of the "new evangelization."

After so many years of being a minister of the word, which especially during my papacy has brought me as a pilgrim to every part of the world, I cannot fail to make further considerations regarding this dimension of priestly life. This is a demanding dimension, since people today look to priests for the "lived" word before they look to them for the "proclaimed" word. The priest must "live by the word." But at the same time, he will try to be *intellectually prepared* to know the word in depth and to proclaim it effectively. In our day, marked as it is by a high degree of specialization in almost all areas of life, intellectual formation is extremely important. Such formation makes it possible to engage in a serious and creative dialogue with contemporary thought. Study of the humanities and of philosophy and a knowledge of theology are the paths to this intellectual formation, which then needs to be continued for the rest of one's life. In order to be authentically formative, study needs to be constantly accompanied by prayer, meditation, and the invocation of the gifts of the Holy Spirit: wisdom, understanding, counsel, fortitude, knowledge, piety, and the fear of the Lord. Saint Thomas Aquinas explains how, with the gifts of the Holy Spirit, a person's whole spiritual being becomes responsive to God's light, not only the light of knowledge but also the inspiration of love. I have prayed for the gifts of the Holy Spirit since my youth, and I continue to do so.

Questions for Pope John Paul II

1. According to John Paul II, what does it mean to be a priest? Explain the importance of holiness, prayer, and study.
2. What is the significance of the Eucharist for the vocation of the ministerial priesthood? How does the priest act "in persona Christi"? Why is the Eucharist so central?
3. Describe what the Pope says about redemption, reconciliation, and the call to holiness.

Index

Adam, 107
ambition, 27, 28, 29, 33, 55, 56, 83
Ambrose, Saint, xv, 35, 110, 111
angels, 104
Antichrist, 21
apostles, 4, 14, 21, 118
apostolic succession, 4, 118, 119, 120
Augustine, Saint, xv, 35, 81, 109, 110
Avignon, 71

baptism, 126
Bernard of Clairvaux, Saint, xv, 51
Bérulle, Cardinal Pierre de, 95
bishops, 4, 5, 12, 119; authority of,
   119, 126, 127; college of, 118, 120,
   121; election of, 67; Episcopal
   duties, 120, 122, 123, 126;
   evangelizing mission, 122, 123,
   124; infallibility, 124, 125;
   obedience owed to, 124;
   ordination of, 120; prelates, 127;
   principle of unity, 122;
   relationship to laity, 69;
   relationship to Pope, 122, 123;

relationship to priests, 119;
   successors of the apostles, 119

cardinal virtues, 52, 53, 54
Catherine of Siena, Saint, xv, 71
charity, 6, 7, 8, 11, 12, 4, 15, 19, 20,
   66, 67, 68, 72, 80, 81, 92, 94, 95,
   100, 125
Cheers television sitcom, xii
Christ. *See* Jesus Christ
church: apostolic, 126; Catholic, x,
   110, 123, 126; composed of sinful
   human beings, x, xii, xiii; disciples
   of Jesus Christ, 12; embodies
   Christ's wisdom, xi, 118;
   established by Christ, 127;
   evangelizing mission, ix, 98, 122,
   123; filled with Holy Spirit, 123,
   127; flock of Christ, 8, 119;
   holiness of, 126; infallibility in
   faith and morals, 124, 125;
   mystical body, 2, 72, 74, 80, 121,
   122, 125; need for continual
   spiritual renewal, xi, xiii; people of

served by ministerial priesthood, 137; submission of faith, 124; unworthiness, x, xii, xiii, 111, 112

priesthood (ministerial): administer the sacraments, 73, 80, 104, 134; authority, 35, 36, 43, 44, 45, 46, 47, 48, 49, 56, 81, 82, 83; called to holiness, xii, xiii, 106, 108, 109, 141, 142; celibacy, 141; danger of pride, 45, 47; dignity, ix, xi, xii, 72, 73, 74, 79; duties of, xi, xii, 3, 29, 65, 80, 127, 134; enduring insults, 30, 31, 100; evangelizing mission, 139, 142; *in persona Christi*, x, 74, 76, 77, 99, 100, 120, 134, 135, 136; intellectual formation, 143; patience, 97, 98, 99, 100, 106, 107; preference for the poor, 37, 142; public reputation, 31, 32; steward, 125, 133, 134, 137, 139, 140; strength comes from God, 100; sympathy with flock, 111, 114, 127; unworthiness, x, xii, 74, 79, 83, 86, 87, 88, 98, 104, 105, 106, 107, 108, 112, 127; vigilance, 86, 127, 139; virtues, 81

providence, 3, 11, 91, 92, 93, 94, 97, 98, 123

purity, 14, 20, 72

sacraments, 79

sacrifice, 8, 13, 81, 99, 100, 134, 135

scandal, xiii, 6

schism, 5, 6, 8

Second Vatican Council, xv, 117, 136, 141

simony, 59, 61, 63

sin, consequences of, 3, 80, 108, 113

Sodomites, 21

suffering, 93, 98, 99

Sulpicians, 97

Thomas Aquinas, Saint, xv, 59, 81, 143

Thomas More, Saint, xv, 85

Valens, 19, 22, 23

zeal, 64

Zechariah, 64

About the Editor

Matthew Levering teaches theology at Ave Maria College in Ypsilanti, Michigan. He is the author of several books, including *Christ's Fulfillment of Torah and Temple* (University of Notre Dame Press), *Knowing the Love of Christ: An Introduction to the Theology of St. Thomas Aquinas* (University of Notre Dame Press, coauthored with Michael Dauphinais), and *Scripture and Metaphysics: Aquinas and the Renewal of Trinitarian Theology* (Oxford: Blackwell, forthcoming).